VIRGIN
TERRITORY

HOW I FOUND
MY INNER GUADALUPE

VIRGIN
TERRITORY

HOW I FOUND
MY INNER GUADALUPE

SUSAN J. COBB

PORSIMISMA PRESS
PUERTO VALLARTA

Published by Porsimisma Press.

Virgin Territory: How I Found My Inner Guadalupe
© 2010 by Susan J. Cobb. All rights reserved.
Printed in the United States of America.

www.susanjcobb.com

First Edition

ISBN 10: 1-4505-8295-8
ISBN 13: 978-1-4505-8295-7

To Larry,
always,
but for now "Lorenzo"

CONTENTS

*In different ages the divine idea assumes different forms,
according to humanity's needs.*

Mary Baker Eddy

*Guadalupe is about God and us—
she redefines us in terms of God,
and God in terms of our most sacred imagery.*

Virgilio Elizondo

Introduction

Mary, Mary, quite contrary. How does your garden grow?
Mother Goose

In late 2006, my husband and I sold practically everything we owned in the States and moved to a little fishing village just north of Puerto Vallarta on the Pacific Coast of Mexico. It was a decision made in a moment of either inspiration or sheer madness. We haven't regretted it for one moment.

Our new home is in a rural area, though visions of a glitzy "Riviera Nayarit" dance in the heads of the governor and of local movers and shakers. It hasn't happened yet in our town. Perhaps with the current economic meltdown, paradise may be safe for a while longer. Life is good here. We've put down roots.

For me, like thousands of other gringos, Mexico these days represents a new beginning. It is definitely "virgin territory" in that sense. But our new beginnings are planted in the dust of ancient civilizations. Vestiges of those who have been here before remain in various forms and practices. Most notable of all is Our Lady of Guadalupe, "Goddess of the Americas." She is an indigenous icon with origins that stretch back thousands of years, and her presence and influence continue to grow stronger both north and south of Mexico's borders. Clothed with the sun, heavy with child, she graces more dashboards, notebook covers, and shopping bags than she does altars in churches. Though appropriated by the Catholic Church, she transcends any religious denomination. For me she is a symbol of all that makes Mexico a haven for women in particular, because Mexico is feminine in so many ways.

First, let me describe the soil from which I was transplanted. I grew up on the plains of West Texas. It's hard to imagine a part of the world, except maybe most of the Middle East, where masculinity seems to permeate even the geography of the place. Maybe it's the flat horizon with razor straight rows of cotton that surrounds Lubbock, or the implacable grid of section line roads turned into urban commerce zones with houses lined up straight and orderly on the alphabetical avenues and numerical streets in between. Windmills, silos, oil derricks, drilling rigs, and fence posts—a veritable forest of phallic symbols—mark the rural terrain. When the Spanish explorer Coronado crossed this area, he found the total lack of landmarks confounding. His expedition took to driving stakes in the ground to mark where they'd been. Hence the name "Llano Estacado," or staked plain. When Larry and I owned a landscape nursery in Midland, more often than not, we had to hire a drilling rig to bore a hole through solid rock just so we could plant a tree. Most trees stand as upright as all the manmade landscape features; no interesting bends or quirks allowed. Older homes in Odessa bear the trademark of an earlier landscape artist: two Italian Cypress sentinels, one anchoring each side of the front door. Further out in the country, the cypress may stand like a string of exclamation points, a barrier against the wind. "Thus far, and no farther!" Their mute warning is clear against a cloudless sky. In West Texas, you always know where people stand, as well. "Fer us or agin us." That stripe down the middle of the very straight road is *yeller*, like the stripe down a coward's back.

In contrast, the landscape in Mexico *undulates*. It rises and falls with intriguing swells and bulges, and someone is always growing something in it. Drop a seed, and in a month's time, there's a tree. Within a year there's fruit. It's a land to get lost in, with roads that dip in and out of valleys and tuck around curves to disappear, then reappear again, offering a totally different view. There is an unconfined amplitude to life here. Houses are constantly being expanded, ready to accommodate new family members, and long-time family members who have wandered are readily forgiven and welcomed home again. Opinions are rarely voiced, and voices rarely raised, except in prayer. When people pray it is usually to the Virgin, not to Jesus, that the prayers are directed.

Protestant Christianity, in general, has not dealt well with the Virgin Mary. It's sort of been, "Thanks for the baby, Lady. Now go get lost." Many Protestants look on her with downright suspicion, like adoptive parents fearful of the claims of a teenaged birth mother. But in Mexico the Virgin, *La Madrecita*, is honored as no other place on earth.

Each year on the evening of December 11, pilgrims converge on the second-most visited Catholic site in the world, the Shrine of Guadalupe. The number grows each year. This past

3

year there were over five million. They come to "watch" with her on the day traditionally celebrated as the anniversary of her appearance to Juan Diego on the hillside of Tepeyac outside of present day Mexico City. Smaller crowds, no less fervent, gather in other parts of the Americas from Anchorage to Tierra del Fuego. Where I live now, this event is celebrated in tiny, makeshift shrines in the dirt streets of La Colonia and La Penita—and it is celebrated exuberantly in Technicolor and surround sound. Evidently Guadalupe *loves* fireworks.

"We're looking for Christmas lights," my Canadian neighbor says, speaking in the clipped, exact tones of her native South Africa. "White ones that *don't* flash."

We've met in the *tianguis*, the Thursday market in La Peñita. It also happens to be the American Thanksgiving Day. "Tupperware Alley" is what gringos call the extension of the market that stretches away from the Indian handwork and colorful displays in the main plaza. Here vendors spread the more mundane items that are needed on a daily basis—plastic dishes, clothespins, pirated DVDs, patent leather sandals, some of the most formidable padded bras I've ever seen, and now, at the end of November, Christmas decorations. There is not a white light to be found. When it comes to decking halls in Mexico, one fact can't be denied: Guadalupe likes *color,* and preferably color that flashes.

Very shortly after we moved to Mexico, both my parents had major health crises. My mother sent my sisters and me notes she'd made for obituaries, both hers and Dad's. My father's ran on for pages. Hers was no more than a paragraph. No more than a paragraph devoted to Mom, who had been the biggest

4

presence in our little lives! Dad may have been physically present with us (though not often), but he always seemed mentally preoccupied with something other than the child before him. Much of that was just the nature of fathering in the 1950s, and much of it had to do with the realization of all those achievements that took up so many pages.

I received Mom's notes when I opened my email the morning after I'd spent the night at a *velada* for Guadalupe. *Velada* comes from the Spanish word for candle, *vela,* and this was an all-night vigil in honor of the Virgin done in the company of friends and loved ones. As I scrolled through the PDF attachment written in my mother's still strong and legible hand, I felt vindicated for our move to Mexico. Here I was in a country that honored La Madre, that told and retold a woman's story, celebrated her appearance each year with hot chocolate and tamales, followed by fireworks at two o'clock in the morning—sharp. Mothers *matter* in Mexico, and Guadalupe is the archetype.

She is an archetype whose origins stretch farther back than the Conquest. The dust of Mexico is heavy with stories of how and when the Virgin has graced humanity with her presence—usually it is in a field to a peasant farmer—and she would like a shrine built, thank you very much. These stories have served the Catholic Church very well in converting an indigenous "pagan" population to a more institutionalized form of worship. But farmers and their conquerors move about on the surface of the earth. Mary's roots go deeper. There is a reason she thrives in Mexico. Beneath the topsoil lie older roots, tenacious and enduring. Entwined in the subterranean consciousness of a modern nation are the tresses of ancient goddesses. Now, transplanted south of the border, every fiber of my being seeks connection to these goddesses. Like roots underground seek out moisture and nutrients, I tap into what they represent. In the process I make contact with something earthy, vital, and nourishing. I hear goddess stories as if they were my own.

Oldest is Coatlicue. Her immense statue dominates a large space in Mexico's Museum of Anthropology. With two serpents as a head, talons for hands, and drooping breasts from nursing her many babies, her image is, to say the least, *formidable.*

Legend has it that Coatlicue gets pregnant by a ball of feathers that fall from a bird as she sweeps her temple on the top of a mountain.

"Don't you hate it when that happens?" interjects my friend Ann, as I tell her this story. She has a tendency towards sarcasm.

"Hush," I respond. "This is a serious legend. It gets better."

Coatlicue's first four hundred children grow jealous when they hear of Mom's condition. Led on by their sister Coyolxauhqui, they get ready to kill the new baby as soon as she "gives it light."

"'Gives it light?'" Ann asks. "What does *that* mean?"

"Dar a luz. It's Spanish for 'to give birth,'" I explain. "The mother brings the baby out of darkness and gives it to the light, see? It's a pretty image, sort of."

Ann shrugs. I have to shrug back. Neither of us have children. What do we know? I continue with the legend.

But a hummingbird tells the baby in Coatlicue's womb what's waiting for him on the outside. So Huitzilopochtli emerges, not as a baby, but fully grown, armed with a sword ("Don't even go there, Ann") ready to defend his mother. He decapitates his sister, tosses her head to the sky where it becomes the moon, and takes his place as ruler.

Ann is silent. Then, "That's one of the most amazing accounts of sibling rivalry I've ever heard." Not everyone appreciates Mexican legends.

Coatlicue is reincarnated through the centuries in a variety of goddess figures. Nowadays there is usually a shrine to the Virgin, in one form or another, wherever one of these goddesses held sway. The most recent incarnation is a distinctly softer, sweeter version, Tonantzín. Tonantzín was the goddess whose temple sat on the promontory above Lake Texcoco when Cortez first gazed across it. Her names were many—Goddess of Sustenance, Honored Grandmother, Mother of the Corn, Mother of the Earth and Creation. Her temple didn't last long after the Conquest. It is now the site of the Capilla, the chapel, which crowns the hill behind the Basilica of our Lady of Guadalupe north of Mexico City.

Is Guadalupe the reincarnation of a pagan goddess? Was her legend promulgated by the Spanish to replace Tonantzín and convert the indigenous population to Roman Catholicism? Or could it be possible, as more recent theories surmise, that the legend of "Our Lady" was created by the indigenous population themselves, to preserve and protect their goddess in a form acceptable to the conquerors? Or, does the image of a woman, clothed in the sun, the moon under her feet, on the verge of delivering a man child whose destroyers stand ready to slay him have a more universal origin and resonance? It's a story handed down in one form or another on every continent, in every culture. We find it today in the Book of Revelation, Chapter 12:

> And there appeared a great wonder in heaven; a woman clothed with the sun, and the moon under her feet, and upon her head a crown of twelve stars; and she being with child cried, travailing in birth, and pained to be delivered. ... and the dragon stood before the woman which was ready to be delivered, for to devour her child as soon as it was born.

Perhaps it is time to "unpack" this ancient feminine archetype, take a fresh look at it, and speculate what message it might have for the twenty-first century. Nineteenth-century religious reformer Mary Baker Eddy wrote about one possibility in a letter dictated to her (male) secretary late in 1900:

> The masculine element has had precedence in history, but the history of time is temporal—it is not eternal. ... The masculine element must not murmur if at some period in human history the verdict should take a turn in behalf of woman, and say,—Her time has come, and the reflection of God's feminine nature is permitted consideration, has come to the front, and will be heard and understood.

With the ascendancy of Guadalupe, perhaps that time has come. She is the plant that tells me of the root beneath. More than any other icon, Guadalupe epitomizes a popular religiosity unconfined to any institution. She is a current symbol of an ancient ethos, a touchstone for what is colorful, primitive, and fundamental to life itself. For me she is a symbol of a universal spiritual ideal, the untapped potential of what lies at the core of every individual. On a personal level, she is the

8

memory of what I once was and what I can yet become, if I am indeed created "in the image of God," a biblical concept that has given grief to women over centuries, in the degree that it has been quoted by men, and taken literally. But Guadalupe is a metaphorical mirror offering an image close to my own, an unmediated experience of divinity that is no longer the privilege of an ordained few or of a specific gender.

In 1810, Mexico's Father Hidalgo raised a flag inscribed with the image of the Virgin of Guadalupe. It encouraged rebellion of the oppressed *mestizos* of Mexico against the despotism of the patrician Spaniards. Guadalupe still symbolizes resistance to "the man," as street gangs and *narco-traficantes* have appropriated her image for their own purposes. I've seen it emblazoned on the forearms of inmates in county jails in Los Angeles and neighboring Orange County. "She's got my back," a young man tells me earnestly, his deep brown eyes contrasting with the orange jumpsuit he wears. He means it literally, referring to the tattoo on that part of his anatomy.

But Guadalupe also provides a rallying point for more creative rebellion across the Americas. For anyone tilling old fields of sterile doctrine and root-bound tradition, she offers fresh mental and spiritual landscapes to explore. For the hurt or wounded, the mentally, physically, or sexually abused, she reflects an image that is unbroken, unharmed, intact—powerful. Heavy with child, she represents new life, a fresh start. And for anyone who longs to claim a unique identity and intrinsic value above and beyond conventional roles and relationships, the Virgin embodies a one-in-herself-ness, which says, *"You* are complete and worthy right now, just the way you are and just because you are."

For anyone who longs for a new spiritual ideal, I dedicate these pages. Welcome to Virgin Territory.

Susan Cobb
Rincón de Guayabitos, Mexico
2009

CHAPTER 1

CALLE SIN SALIDA

Behold, I will do a new thing;
now it shall spring forth; shall ye not know it?
I will even make a way in the wilderness, and rivers in the desert.
Isaiah

Calle Sin Salida. It was a green sign high on a utility pole at a corner where one cobblestone street met another. The plaque was framed in orange stephanotis that dripped from the electric lines like tropical icicles. *Calle Sin Salida*—not the name of the street itself, but rather a warning: "Street without an exit." In English, *dead end.*

Below that plaque there was another, printed with the actual name: Calle Golondrinas. My husband and I had been wandering through a neighborhood of bird names for streets— *Pelicanos, Gaviotas, Pavo Real, Colibri:* Pelicans, Seagulls, Peacocks, Hummingbirds. I'd looked them up as we went along.

This street was Golondrinas: "Swallows Street." I knew that because we lived at the time near California's San Juan Capistrano, famous for its swallows and its Spanish heritage. No translation needed for us on this one. The words were neatly centered above another line of printing: "La Islita Pizza" and a local telephone number. Big cities in the States have corporate sponsors for their stadiums. Rural Mexico has sponsors for their street signs.

My husband gripped the steering wheel more firmly and downshifted. Driving over cobblestones isn't conducive to conversation, and this particular street was teeth-jarringly picturesque.

"Let's see how close we can get to the beach," Larry ventured. "I'll bet this road leads right to it."

Not a bad bet, as shortly after the entrance to the street, we crossed a little bridge and caught a glimpse of the waves and sand beyond. We took our time, taking in the houses, the gardens, and the glimpses of bright beckoning blue between them.

My surf-loving husband was on a quest to see how close to the ocean he could find a house. I was along for the ride of what I was sure was pure folly. We had spent ten days of a two-week vacation exploring the Nayarit coast north of Puerto Vallarta, playing lookie-loo with real estate agents from Sayulita north to La Peñita. We were halfway serious about buying a second home, mostly dreaming and what-if-ing. It was February 2006, and we were mostly just tired, glad to be away from the electric atmosphere of coastal Southern California. We were worn out from work that had become repetitive, and the mental tension of an election-year America polarized into opposing factions. Half of our friends were too despondent to talk; the other half, too excited and gung-ho not to stop.

What an amazing change of pace we'd found 1,500 miles south on the Pacific Coast of mainland Mexico. "Changes in latitude, changes in attitude," as the song goes. Much further back in my life I'd had a brief career—six years worth—selling houses in that frenetic market north of the border. Your reputation and livelihood depended on getting back to people, the sooner the better, striking while the buyers were hot and the sellers were willing to move. Not the case in this place. We'd been trying to connect with someone—anyone—who could show us property in Guayabitos. It never happened. Left to our own devices we cruised around, assessing not only the houses to which we did manage to gain access, but our own prospects for the future. We both felt physically and mentally spent, not dead yet, but barely living. We sensed rather than knew that we'd reached a major turning point in our lives. We were ready for a change, open to it. We just didn't know what it would look like.

"There's the beach," Larry announced.

We had reached the end of the road and stopped in the cul-de-sac. We were facing north, and to the left of us stretched the deep blue Pacific, embraced by the long sandy arms that defined Jaltemba Bay. Smack in the middle of the bay sat a small island that looked like half an over-sized hairy coconut. Straight beyond our windshield lay a stretch of flowing water, the river dividing Rincón de Guayabitos from La Peñita. Here it entered the bay between two rock groins that stretched out into the water providing a passage for fishing boats. At the end of the groin on our side of the river, facing down the waves, there was a cross. But more than a cross. *Is that a shrine of some sort?* I wondered, making a mental note to check it out later.

13

Directly in front of us, across the river were buildings. From a cantina we could hear the plaintive *aaay pobre corazón* music. There was what looked like a small apartment house with a *palapa* shade structure on top. Broadleaf *guayaba* trees lined a rock embankment, their deep green reflected in the water. *Guayabitos* was the diminutive form of the tree, or its fruit, for which the town was named. There were also palms, more shaggy fringed *palapas,* and ruffles of red tile roofs. If there had been a bridge, we could have crossed to what looked like an extension of this cobblestone street. Ah, but it was *Calle Sin Salida.* The end of the road. There was no access from here to there. The village across the water was just far enough away to be mysterious and quaint.

To our right, we peered past a hedge of brilliant bougainvillea and took in the white plaster walls of what looked to be a large home. It had a scroll of an iron gate in front of a courtyard. The red tiled roof that slanted slightly down towards us was not a faraway ruffle. We were close enough to see its tip-tilty planes, topped with a big white dome pierced with clerestory windows. Rising above the dome was an honest-to-gosh cupola. I couldn't tell if the house had one story, two, three, or maybe a mixture of them all. The structure was set back from the street but at an elevation that, from where we were in the car, I could see a man sitting on what looked like a front porch or balcony. He was having a cup of coffee, looking out at the ocean—and at us. He waved. I waved back, and he rose, starting down the broad brick staircase that led from the front entrance of the house to the curvy iron gate.

"I think he's coming out to talk to us!" I said.

14

Larry turned the car around and headed out of the cul-de-sac, stopping so the man could lean against the driver's side. He indeed wanted to talk.

Leaning into the window of the small rental car, he got right to the point: "You folks wanna buy a house? This one's for sale." He pointed to a small sign on the front gate, which I now remembered catching a glimpse of as we'd passed. We'd been too enthralled with the view before us to take much notice.

"Hmmmm. Maybe." Larry was non-committal. We'd been around the area. We knew the prices. This house looked way out of our league.

The guy named a price. We were right. Definitely more than we wanted to spend for a second home. I said so.

Not to be put off, he asked, "Where you folks from?"

"California," I responded. "San Clemente."

"Us, too!" He waved toward the house, indicating someone else inside, and reeled off an address. It was about two miles from where we were currently living in the States. "Left about sixteen years ago. Own your home there?"

I knew what was happening. We were being pre-qualified, but it was gentle, friendly. I had the feeling we were in the hands of a master. We talked about San Clemente and its neighboring towns of Dana Point and San Juan Capistrano, living near water, when was the best time of year, when was it lousy. Ultimately—who could resist his invitation "come on in and have a look"? No longer was he "a guy." He was Jim.

Right from the start, we knew this was not your bare-bones tropical resort-style residence. Mexican modern it was not. Well over thirty years old, the house was venerable for the area, with construction details that spoke its age. Walls almost a foot thick splayed into even larger footprints below in the basement. Well, it wasn't really a *basement*. The bottom floor of the house was only half underground. This is what gave it a higher elevation than its neighbors, and accounted for the broad sweeping staircase leading up to the main entrance. What was below was a subterranean red-tiled space that wandered like a great cavern under the entire house. At present it was packed solid with "a few of our things," Jim said airily. But we could see there was ample room for multiple vehicles, a laundry room, a workshop/tool room, a garden supply area, a place for pool equipment, and lots of storage area left over.

But it was the house above that worked its magic on us. One pass through it, and Larry and I had a sneaky suspicion. No, it was a conviction. *This was it.*

First of all there was the kitchen. It was spacious, and at one end French doors opened street side onto the small balcony/ porch where I'd first seen our "guy." I wanted to sit there, too, and watch the world go by. Inside there was a breakfast area and a large tiled island supporting a six-burner gas range and room enough to set up a buffet meal. Along one side of the room, the counter holding the sink and prep area looked out across the river to the inaccessible village. The other end of the kitchen was defined by a bank of dark wood cabinets, a deep pantry and open shelves. *"Huanacaxtle* wood," Jim explained. He stroked the pantry door. "Absolutely termite-resistant."

There was more of it through the house: solid core raise-paneled doors opened to high-ceilinged rooms. Dark louvered doors hid closets and cabinets. This house had storage! There was a pervasive formal air, a colonial sort of elegance that spoke brandy snifters rather than margaritas. We stopped near the tiled alcove in the front hallway. I looked puzzled. *Why would anyone put a sink here?*

As if divining my thought, Jim explained. "Guy that built the house had a few little quirks. He was a television producer. Came up with some game show that really hit it big. Had an eye for details, though. Some of them are a little screwy."

Our flip-flops slapped against cool ceramic tile floors, a mottled pattern that resembled white sand at low tide. Above, red brick *boveda* ceilings arched gracefully at varying elevations, sometimes bursting into *glorieta* designs where the walls were curved. The ceiling in the kitchen rose to a peak of over twelve feet above the tile-topped island. One in a spare bedroom hovered over a reading alcove at a much cozier level. There were niches and crenellations and unexpected angles and curves wherever we turned.

The interior should have been dark, but it wasn't. Right in the heart of the house there was a great open roundness filled with light. The cupola room sat directly beneath the tiered dome that had caught our attention from the street. Post-meridian sunbeams skittered across the tiles and splashed up on white plaster walls. Intuitively I knew the potential of this space. It should be filled, but with what, I wasn't certain. For now it was completely empty, a glorified hallway between the entrance and the verandah beyond. *Had Jim and his wife ignored this room because it had no view to the outside?* I looked up at the clerestory windows that admitted the sunlight. I could imagine looking at the moon through those windows. This was a room for reflection in every sense of the word.

"It's like a house in a mystery story," I breathed aloud.

"Oh, it's a house with a history, all right," responded Jim quickly. He was a little hard of hearing. "It was built by that TV guy, and he sold it to a drug lord. That guy was shot right here in the living room. His best friend and partner did it. He's in prison now. The next guy who bought it was a soldier of fortune. He found a stash of $40,000 in the ceiling there above the hallway. Probably drug money. Come on through to the back. I'll show you where they used to toss the sacks of drugs from the *estero,* over the wall into the swimming pool."

Was he kidding? Larry and I looked at each other and followed wordlessly.

The first thing we saw behind the house was not the swimming pool but the river. Here, obscured from the street by the house, the river split, forming a tree-covered island that sat a stone's throw off the back of the property. Reflected in the water was a flock of white egrets settling in the palms that studded the islet. From the verandah where we stood, a flight of stairs led downward to a blue-tiled swimming pool, just steps from the back of the house. Beyond that there was a broad deck, an open barbeque cabana, and a low iron rail fence built back from a rock embankment.

"I built the deck and cabana," Jim said proudly. "Also that rock wall between here and the river. Carried those stones out of the mountains. Before, there was a concrete wall right up next to the pool. About eight feet tall. Made it really private, but blocked the view. I guess there was a reason, though. The speed boats would come in close after dark, and up and over the walls would go the bags—right into the pool."

"Bags of what?" I asked. "Marijuana? Opium poppies?" The hills of rural Nayarit would seem to lend themselves to all manner of illegal agriculture.

"Oh, I'm not sure," Jim hedged. "Marijuana, maybe. Maybe money! I don't know how they worked it. Just know the guy who lived here, that was his business."

Jim's story obviously had a few kinks to work out. I thought he probably told it strictly for the romantic cachet it lent to his pitch for selling the house.

The pool was large but so close to the house we couldn't see it when we sat down on the verandah half a story above it. I could imagine diving directly into it without even having to go outside. It was inviting, but not enchanting. It was the verandah itself that worked its spell on me. Ten feet deep it stretched across the rear of the building. It was cool, private, and shielded from the afternoon sun. Two ceiling fans kept the air moving over tropical furniture beneath. I half-expected to see Somerset Maugham rise and greet us. The curve of the river seemed to embrace the house. Where drug runners may have plied the water, now there were fishing skiffs that zoomed around the island and skimmed the surface of the river directly behind the back fence, startling the egrets, as well as pelicans and roseate spoonbills from their own fishing business. They rose in squawking clouds of protest each time it happened.

Across the length of the verandah, four deep-silled arches framed the view. I mentally stuffed them with potted geraniums. From a swinging *hamaca* chair, I would be able to see it all: *estero*, palms, hills in the distance with the suggestion of structures and civilization. And behind it all lay the backdrop of mountains.

I knew those mountains. I tend to anthropomorphize landscapes, and I like to know the given names of topographical features. It's like knowing who your neighbors are. These mountains were the Sierra Vallejo, a small chain of the grander and more extensive Sierra Madre Occidental. *Sierra Madre:* Mother mountains. The double peaks of the Sierra Vallejo rise behind Guayabitos, like Saddleback Mountain rises over South Orange County, California.

I'm not the only one prone to anthropomorphizing land forms. I was to find out later that local fishermen call the Sierra Vallejo "Dolly Parton," a much more descriptive term. I could relate. Twenty years before, we had moved from the flat plains of West Texas to the area around San Juan Capistrano. I nestled into the foothills of that *sierra* like a child at its mother's bosom. But life around Saddleback Mountain had become hectic and harried. I no longer had time to nestle. Here, with nature literally at my doorstep instead of far beyond some freeway, I was ready to nuzzle in and be nurtured.

Jim knew how to talk a good story. He also knew when to fall quiet. For a while we sat in silence, listening to the birds, the fishing boats, the sound of traffic from the distant highway, the *thwump, thwump* of the ceiling fans above. Gradually I became aware of another sound, an underlying rhythm. It was not as pervasive as the freeway noise that enveloped our house in California, but it was definitely a presence. Resonant, it wrapped the whole house like a *rebozo* wraps a baby. I listened to identify it. Surf!

Out of sight here at the back of the house, the ocean still made its presence known, constant as a heartbeat. Throbbing. Continuous. Consoling. "Nestle in," it seemed to say. "Be safe. Be still. You're home."

The conversation Larry and I had that night was basically a mutual confirmation of what we both knew we were going to do. No second home, this house on Calle Golondrinas. It was home. "We'll take it," we told Jim the next day, and we wrote out a sales contract on a yellow legal pad. *Calle Sin Salida* may have been a street without an exit, but for us, it looked like a way out.

STARTING WITH WHITE

The first thing I did to the interior of the house was paint the inside of the round-arched windows on the verandah. It was a territorial act of claiming possession. Jim's wife Janet had scrupulously painted every surface within her reach white. Thank God she was short and couldn't reach the shiny brick cornices that defined most of the outside doors. But a flat matte finish obscured the original color of the balusters and wide sills of the verandah balustrade. Decorative terracotta relief that framed windows and entries had received similar treatment. All the detailed ornamentation had been painted over, now distinguishable from the surrounding white walls only by the dust that had collected on them.

I directed handyman Chano with his paintbrush and ladder: cerulean blue for the arches, deep Indian red for the balusters, the sills, and the tiny tile eyebrows that echoed the form of the arches.

No da color. No pinta. "Doesn't have color," "doesn't paint" are Mexican expressions meaning the inability to define oneself or to take needed action. So in painting the arches, I began putting a new face on our house. Little did I know it was the start of re-defining who I was, as well. Blue arches and dozens of potted geraniums—purple, hot pink, coral and deep red—it was a good place to begin.

CHAPTER 2

SAYING YES:
LE POINT VIERGE

And Mary said,
Behold the handmaid of the Lord; be it unto me according to thy word.
Luke

In retrospect, maybe buying the house on such an impulse wasn't the wisest way to do things. But, when you're in quicksand, even the back of an alligator looks inviting. It didn't take long for us to find that the charming log we'd jumped onto was not all it appeared to be. I've had friends say, "Why don't you write a book about how to buy a house in Mexico?" Well, the way we bought our house is *not* the way I would recommend anyone doing it—ever. If there were a film made of the whole process, it should have a caption running along the bottom, like in those advertisements for what sports cars can do, saying, "These are professional drivers. Do not attempt to duplicate these actions." Only we weren't professional anything. We were just ready to say "yes." And somehow, we "knew."

Was it that interior knowledge, that one-in-herself authority, that inspired Mary of Nazareth to say "yes" to the big change in her life? Confronted by an angel who tells her about this change-the-course-of the-world process in which she's going to be involved, the birth of Jesus, she says, "Behold, the handmaid of the Lord!" No hesitation. No, "But I wanted *Joseph's* baby!" No wondering, *What are Mom and Dad going to say? Could I have some time to think about this?* None of that. Just "yes." At the core of her being, did she know this was something meant to be? Perhaps she acted from what twentieth-century monk Thomas Merton would centuries later describe as *le point vierge:*

> At the center of our being is a point of nothingness which is untouched by sin and by illusion, a point of pure truth, a point or spark which belongs entirely to God, which is never at our disposal, from which God disposes our lives, which is inaccessible to the fantasies of our own mind or the brutalities of our own will. This little point of nothingness and of absolute poverty is the pure glory of God in us.

"Nothingness and absolute poverty." That about sums up where Larry and I were mentally when we came to the house on Calle Golondrinas. We had reached the end of our rope when we came to the end of that road. There by the river, the ocean at our backs, the mountains before us, surrounded by a house that seemed to welcome us with open arms, we said "Yes."

For over forty years Larry and I have always agreed on the big stuff of life. (Deciding where to eat out on a Friday night is a whole other story.) This mutual "knowing" of the significant has been a hallmark of our partnership. Maybe it's because we grew up together. Not from-the-cradle growing up, but changing from adolescents-into-adults growing up. I was seventeen and an old-fashioned virgin when we met. And

24

Larry, two years my senior, was a virgin, as well. Steeped in religious training, we were both excruciatingly "good" children. Good and inexperienced.

The most rebellious thing Larry ever did was join the Air Force at the height of the Vietnam war. The most rebellious thing I ever did was marry him. And even then, as a concession to my parents, I waited until three weeks after my twentieth birthday so I wouldn't be a "teenage bride." "Teen marriages are doomed to failure," my mom insisted. I'm not sure that those three weeks made the difference, but Larry and I are still together with no immediate plans for changing things.

Allowing myself to be chosen and loved extravagantly was a new and transforming experience. Never before had I been *courted*. Larry Cobb pursued me as if I were a treasure. Each weekend, he arrived at the front door with a flower. "That boy can make a dozen roses stretch for months," was the only comment my father made. Well, he was doing it on a U.S. Air Force airman's paltry salary. Every penny was allotted for a purpose. Car payments and insurance on his '56 VW took up the major portion.

There was enough left over for four weekend dates where actual money was spent—if we took in the movie on base. Admission there was a fifty cents instead of two dollars in town. They were first run movies—you just had to stand for the national anthem before the film started rolling. The rest of our time was spent hanging out—in his car, in my parents' living room, and, when at last I moved out of my parents house and into the dormitory at Texas Tech, we hung out in a very public television room, one of the few co-ed spaces provided in student housing. This was in an era when men weren't allowed in the women's living quarters upstairs. Nor, for that matter, were personal televisions. It was in deference to protecting privacy and personal space for residents—archaic concepts today.

There were few places we could be alone, so nothing was more natural than when he "officially" proposed—one of the many times he did so even though I was always saying yes, yes, yes—it was in a very public space. He wrote it large in bright yellow paint on the construction site fence surrounding the new Language Arts building: "Susan Jackson! Will you marry me?" And for a whole semester every time I was introduced or my name was called in class, someone would ask me, "Are you going to marry that guy?" Yes. Yes. Yes!

We had the ceremony in Bowman Chapel at the First Methodist Church in downtown Lubbock, oblivious to what else was happening on August 15, 1969. Neither of us would even hear of Woodstock until they made the movie several years later. It was a Methodist church because the Church of Christ, Scientist, the denomination in which we were both raised, doesn't have ordained clergy. Oddly enough, the *Church Manual* governing members of The Mother Church provides that Christian Scientists be married by ordained clergy, so sticking to "the rules," we skipped looking for a justice of the peace and went in search of a denomination that would accommodate us.

My mother was raised in the Baptist church and most of the family who would be attending was still Baptist, so that's where we went first. It was harder than we thought. Seems the pastors of those churches wanted you to actually be a Baptist if you were going to be married there. I got the feeling the two of us were infected with spiritual cooties of some kind. At last, my college roommate suggested a professor at Texas Tech, an ordained Methodist minister who taught a course in family relations. Score! We met in a short series of interviews, and he agreed to perform the ceremony. Now that we had a minister, we had an "in" for finding a church—a Methodist church.

Southern Baptists outnumber Methodists by about a jillion to one in Lubbock. I do not lie when I say I think there are more Baptist churches on the High Plains of Texas than there are gas stations. I know one small town of under 1,200 that supports three of them, plus two Churches of Christ, a Pentecostal congregation, and a Catholic church. First Baptist Church in Lubbock rises like a megalithic monument surrounded by a campus that seems to expand every time I return to my birthplace. It now covers three square city blocks. It's the largest Southern Baptist congregation in the world. And, just to assure Lubbock's place in the pantheon of big Baptist churches, Second Baptist Church, Lubbock, is the second largest Baptist church in the world. So if some Islamist terrorist plot blows the really big church off the face of the earth, or if the limestone caprock the town is built on should open up and one megalith should sink into another, Second Baptist Church would be right there waiting to take up the slack.

By contrast, First Methodist Church, farther downtown on the same street, is noted not for the size of its congregation but the refinement of its Gothic architecture and adornments, including a rose window, one of the four largest in the world,

27

to rival the one in Notre Dame. That's Notre Dame in Paris, not Notre Dame in Indiana. The main sanctuary at First Methodist, in addition to the rose window, was chock full of stained glass and ecclesiastical class. It was beautiful, but much too large for our needs. We chose the smaller chapel, where we could still take advantage of the church reception parlor. This was elegantly carpeted in contrast to the utilitarian linoleum tile of First Baptist. There was also a grand piano and a fireplace. Methodists, like Presbyterians, usually have excellent taste. I always try to make their rummage sales.

We had a friend who would play contemporary music during the reception on the white grand piano by the fireplace with the white mantel. That had been another Baptist no-no. Secular songs were strictly verboten in church buildings, even the love themes from all those great 1960s movies. So while the pianist segued from *The Shadow of Your Smile* to *Lara's Theme,* guests could choose between the two cakes—the traditional bride's cake and—a more recent innovation—a groom's cake made of darker batter. West Texas trend-setters that we were, we decided against chocolate for Larry's cake, opting for a more modern coffee-flavored confection. It was pre-Starbuck's and pretty tame, but at least it was brown. Besides the cakes there were salted peanuts and an un-spiked pink fruit punch. That was pretty much the extent of Protestant wedding celebrations in West Texas. The fancier affairs would opt for adding little white cream-cheese sandwiches, but we provided pink butter mints instead.

Pink was the theme for just about everything at that wedding—except for my dress. That was white—white, white, white, white, white—with a big V for Virgin-shaped train that

28

stretched halfway down the aisle of the small chapel. There was an inverted V of lace that touched the base of my throat in front and proceeded to make me break out in hives of nervous anticipation. I was more than a blushing bride. I was inflamed. Hemphill-Wells was "the" department store in town. With the purchase of my wedding gown came a wedding consultant, and half an hour before I was to walk down the aisle the High Plains arbiter of tasteful affairs, Juanita MacDivitt, was tucked under my chin tacking soft velvet behind the offending brocade.

I look at the photos now and see how desperately my dad and I leaned against each other as we came down the aisle. Perhaps he was being protective, but I also needed the guidance. I couldn't see two feet in front of me. I had decided against wearing my tortoise shell, slanty cat-eye glasses. Even though they were in style—well, sort of—I thought they might "date" the photos. It was my day, and gosh darn it, I was going to look *perfect*.

It was several years later that I finally acquiesced to getting contact lenses. I'd always been touchy about someone coming at me with a pointed finger, and had always promptly fainted before the contact lens had entered my eye. But when my cousin Phil, a newly minted optometrist, offered to have patience with me if I'd have patience with him, I decided to give them a try. I was appalled when he told me as I sat in his exam chair, glasses in my lap, "You might want to put those glasses back on. They'll keep that right eye from crossing." Could it have been? No, surely not. I couldn't have gone through my whole wedding with my eyes crossed! Certainly someone would have said *something*, right? The photos tell me nothing. Like

Guadalupe, I was demure, eyes cast downward and to the side. Rarely did I look squarely into the camera that day.

Larry and I left the chapel in a flurry of rice and a garishly decorated '63 Ford Fairlane, successor to the VW Bug that had died a few months before on a Farm to Market Road by an irrigation ditch. We drove all the way to a motel on the outskirts of Lubbock, Donny Anderson's Red Raider Inn. It was owned by and named for a then-famous former football player at Texas Tech. The bridal suite was called "Helmet House." The first thing we did was order chicken-fried steaks and mashed potatoes from room service, sit in bed, and watch television. Alone at last! And we were scared spit-less.

This is not a book about my coming of age or discovering the wonders of being a woman. Dear Reader, are you disappointed? Well, we were. Disappointed, that is. It *wasn't* magic. It *wasn't* roses, trumpets, and fireworks then. It definitely got better, but for something that was supposed to be such a big deal, it seemed like a lot of hard work at first. And when at last the deed was done, I was still just Susan. Same old Susan and same old Larry. What has really mattered over these forty years or so is the day to day life living with the same old Larry. That's been transformational. It still is. But now, looking back, I have a few thoughts about that whole *virgin* thing.

Being a virgin had always seemed such a negative to me, like I was living in the land of something that hadn't happened yet. It was a state to be ridiculed by classmates and speculated on by the formidable groups of football players that hung out in the corridors of Coronado High School. I went to great lengths to avoid passing those groups, hugging my books to a very flat chest, my eyes glued to the linoleum in front of me.

Virgin. From the lips of mid-'60s teenagers, the word was an epithet. Untouched, inexperienced, *never had sex.* Even the more positive dictionary definitions of the word weren't particularly helpful: modest, chaste, pure. It was as if *virgin* were something not fully formed, a state of suspended being. Waiting. Passive. Admittedly, in high school I wasn't analyzing my virginity in any deeper way then wondering how I was going to lose it. Now on the cusp of my wedding, it was as if those around me were surprised that it could possibly happen.

"You? Getting married?" My former high school English teacher shrieked with astonishment. She'd called to see if I could house sit or something. I told her about my other plans for that particular August weekend. After her initial outburst, she began laughing. "Well," she chuckled, "I guess anything is possible!" I had never really liked her.

After all, she didn't know me. No one did. Not really. I was a secret even to myself.

But I wanted to be known—known, yes, in the Biblical sense, like, "And Adam knew Eve, and she conceived." That was a start. But even more, I had a hunger for deeper intimacy—to be known like in the Psalm, "O Lord, you've searched me and known me." And, "Behold, you want truth in the inward parts: and in the hidden part thou shalt make me to know wisdom." In *The Message Bible,* Eugene Peterson translates this last as, "What you're after is truth from the inside out. Enter me, then; conceive a new, true life." Being entered physically is one thing, but being entered down to your heart's core is a whole different kind of knowledge. It would be like becoming one with what conceived me in the first place—and there's space enough in that knowledge to explore a world, a universe.

Conception unconfined. Openness to new things. Hunger for something more than a life lived in carefully prescribed channels. I didn't recognize my virginity for what it was— authority to go forward. Esther Harding's *Woman's Mysteries: Ancient and Modern* points out that in ancient times the word virgin had a different meaning than it does now. It didn't mean being chaste or physically untouched. Rather, being a virgin meant "belonging to oneself." A virgin was someone who had authority, who was the author of her own experience, not defined by any human relationship. Virginity was power. Being a virgin, she says, refers to "a quality, a subjective state, a psychological attitude, not to be a physiological or external fact." It means being uncaptured or, as Harding puts it, a virgin is "one-in-herself."

I didn't know any of that then, but there was one thing I did know. I no longer "belonged" to my parents. But I didn't "belong" to Larry Cobb either. The authority I exerted in saying "yes" came from a place more in the heart than the hormones. Larry was a place where I knew I'd be safe. I knew he thought I was smart, and that he'd always support that, encourage it. He himself was smart, but he wasn't book smart. Plagued with dyslexia, reading was never a joy for him. However, I knew that if he and I were stranded on a desert island, he'd put me under a tree, give me a book, and go kill lunch. Or build a tree house. Or construct some sort of flying or sailing machine that would get us off the stupid island. Whatever he did, I wanted to be there with him while he did it. And amazingly, he wanted me there with him. Learning to receive his love, I was beginning to open up to all life's possibilities. So I moved toward marriage with a determination that I have since rarely shown in moving toward anything—until we moved to Mexico.

My decision to marry was about being me, getting out, getting away, and fulfilling my own particular destiny and purpose. I felt the same strong impetus about our move south of the border. Once again I was cutting family ties and taking on the mantle of becoming something more than I'd been before. Maybe the mark of a real virgin is she says "Yes!"

BREAKING AND ENTERING
AND THE NEED FOR PROTECTION

"There's always the first time, and it's usually the last."

Counsel from neighbors, long-time residents who have been around a while. We'd been burglarized. Not robbed, which means a face-to-face confrontation. No, this was classic leave-the-house-unguarded and come-back-to-find-it-rifled. For burglars, they were extraordinarily polite. The glass louvers on the bedroom window had been carefully removed and stacked neatly on the tile floor of the verandah—our beautiful, open, and airy verandah—before the screen was removed and the burglars stepped inside to pilfer anything small, gold, and valuable.

They didn't find much. Our real valuables had been sequestered in the secret safe room. But the sense of having been violated affected Larry deeply, suffering as he was from culture shock and lack of language during those first weeks of living in Mexico. He was determined not to have it happen again.

Enter Leo, welder extraordinaire, and the first link in what would become an expanding network of contractor contacts—the kind of guys Larry loves having around him. I love them, too. They fix things. And so began a month long project of erecting wrought-iron protection over every available entrance. The verandah remained open and airy, but access to the main house could now be shut off with long sliding barred gates across the two main bedroom doors. We painted them to match our mood of the perceived necessity—*violeta profunda*—deep purple.

CHAPTER 3

A FEW WORDS
ABOUT MARY

For it was Mary, Mary, long before the fashion changed.
George M. Cohan

My mother-in-law's name was Chloe, a name that was not so common when she got it in 1926. But her mother was named Mary, one of the most common names of all. In fact Chloe's aunts were named Marie and Marian. There is a family photo of these three flapper sisters sitting on a split rail fence, showing a lot of leg and smoking cigarettes while four-year-old Chloe looked on. That was the same year Mary, Marie, and Marian were arrested in Long Beach for making gin in a bathtub. They were rowdy girls, even for Southern California.

There are a lot of Marys in the Bible, and they were rowdy girls, too. Beginning in Exodus, there's Miriam, whose name is a form of Mary. She was Moses' big sister, who watched over her little brother until he was taken safely out of the Nile and installed in Pharaoh's palace. Later, on the trip out of Egypt, she wasn't afraid to tell the same little brother, he who had parted the Red Sea, was leading an exodus of thousands,

35

and would be depicted centuries later in epic proportions by Charlton Heston and Val Kilmer, exactly what she thought about his new wife—an Ethiopian, a *black* woman. Never mind that older brother Aaron shared the same politically incorrect opinion. It was Miriam who got leprosy and seven days exile from the camp. No wonder her name, the root of the name "Mary," means "bitter."

Then there was Naomi, who adopted the name. "Don't call me Naomi," she said, on returning to her hometown of Bethlehem and being greeted by kinfolk and neighbors who hadn't seen her for ages. "Call me 'Mara,' because God has dealt bitterly with me." Naomi/Mara was the mother-in-law of Ruth, the biblical Ruth of "Entreat me not to leave thee, or return from following after thee, for whither thou goest, I will go" fame. Even though the words make great wedding vows, they were spoken by a daughter-in-law to her mother-in-law. The mother-in-law in question, Naomi/Mara, had not only lost her husband, but her two sons as well, a total disaster for a Hebrew woman of that era. What she was left with was a foreign daughter-in-law tagging along behind her. She saw herself as a woman handed a raw deal indeed, so she identifies herself with that place of bitter waters in the desert that Miriam before her knew so well.

Jumping ahead a few centuries, we find a whole slew of Marys in the New Testament. There's the Virgin Mary's sister-in-law, also named Mary. Or could she have been the Virgin's sister? Authorities are unclear, hesitant to think that two sisters could bear the same name. Perhaps they never met my mother-in-law's grandfather. Whatever the relationship, Mary of Clopas is called "the other Mary," and she shows up from time to time in the Biblical narrative because two of her sons are disciples of Jesus. Jesus' Aunt Mary was not above promoting the welfare of these two boys, asking straight out if cousin Jesus wouldn't see fit to put one on the right hand and one on the left in that kingdom he was supposed to establish. "After all, Jesus, they're family!"

There's a woman of independent means named Mary, who was also the mother of a young boy named John whose surname was Mark. John Mark, being a little kid who hadn't yet reached the age of twelve, was not part of the disciples' team, but Peter let him hang around. Besides, John Mark's mother had a house big enough to accommodate the first groups of Christians, and a willingness to let them meet there. Little John Mark grew up to write the Gospel of Mark, which starred Jesus, but gave a major supporting role to Peter. So thanks to that Mary, we have John Mark's up-close-and-personal account of the life of Jesus, an account that is also the first and oldest of the four Gospels.

There's also Mary, the sister of Martha and Lazarus. The three siblings lived in Bethany, outside of Jerusalem, and often had Jesus as a guest in their home. Of course, Mary and Martha would be cooking in the kitchen and serving the meal. Lazarus, Jesus, and any other men around would be out front in what passed for a living room, sitting around talking, but mostly probably listening to what Jesus had to say. Then one day it happened. Mary got fed up with the job in the kitchen and had the audacity to leave. In she came and sat right down in the middle of everything, right at the feet of Jesus, where she listened intently. Did she dare at that time to ask questions, or was her presence alone enough to challenge the rabbi?

No one recorded her words, but we remember what her sister said. We can almost hear Martha, "cumbered about much serving," issuing a self-righteous appeal: "Don't you care that my sister has left me to serve alone?" But it wasn't Mary that Jesus corrected. Jesus told Martha that it was Mary who was doing the right thing. She had chosen the "good" part, and it wasn't going to be taken away from her. Hooray for Jesus! Hooray for Mary! And, what's more, Mary kept on choosing that good part. Not too long after, this very same Mary antagonized the group of male disciples who followed Jesus. She was "wasteful," breaking open a box of extravagantly expensive spikenard paste to anoint the feet of her friend and rabbi before his last fateful (and fatal) entrance into Jerusalem. "Spendthrift woman," they said. "That money could have been better spent feeding the poor." But, as always, Mary knew what she was doing. Could she in fact be the woman apostle, the "Apostle to the Apostles," who is now known as Mary Magdalene? Again, no surprise, authorities are divided.

But modern scholarship now holds one thing for certain: Mary Magdalene was not the foot-washing "strange woman," a biblical euphemism for "whore," who dared to crash a dinner party and come in behind the sofa where Jesus, again a dinner guest, was reclining. This time it was not among friends or disciples, but in the home of a hoity-toity Pharisee. Very rich people back then ate lying down—one ancient Middle Eastern custom that I for one would happily be willing to incorporate into present day Western society. But there in the midst of what was certainly, again, an all-male gathering of well-to-do movers and shakers, to the embarrassment and consternation of the host, this "sinner" proceeded to literally let down her hair, cry on Jesus' feet, and then wipe them with her long tresses.

Any one of these activities, carried out in so open a way between a man and a woman, would have been cause for scandal. It certainly called into question the judgment of Jesus. Didn't this rabbi know who was touching him? But no one interrupted her. Did Jesus have his hand up? Did he freeze-frame any reaction with a raised eyebrow? She finished her public display of contrition and affection by breaking open a bottle of oil and thoroughly bathing his feet with the contents. It was the early Church that equated this "strange woman" with Mary Magdalene and held her up as an object lesson in assertive humility, while at the same time discrediting the Magdalene's legitimate role as a disciple by associating her with a prostitute. In Mark's Gospel, it is recorded that it is Mary Magdalene who is the first to see Jesus after the cross. She brings the news of his resurrection to the mourning disciples. They don't believe her. Was it to justify their lack of credulity that she is said to have been once possessed of seven devils? That would be one way to solve "a problem like Maria."

But surpassing all the Mary's on record, there was *the* Mary, the mother of Jesus, the *Virgin* Mary—Virgin with a capital "V." The Greek word *parthenos,* which is translated "virgin," can mean simply "young girl," but as she was "espoused" to an older man Joseph, we can assume that as the story begins she is probably a virgin in the physical sense of the word in addition to all her other "virgin" qualities. Matthew says she was "found with child of the Holy Ghost." The symbol of the Holy Ghost is often depicted as a dove, which would parallel the story of Coatlicue being impregnated by a ball of feathers. However it happens, as soon as this particular *parthenos* receives the news of her pregnancy, she doesn't tell her parents. She goes off to visit her much older cousin Elizabeth.

Elizabeth is much, *much* older. In fact Elizabeth and her husband Zacharias are senior citizens by New Testament standards. Zacharias is a priest. Several months before Mary's visit, Zacharias was doing whatever it is high priests do when they enter the holy of holies, the secret chamber behind the altar in the temple, and he gets a visit from an angel with a surprising piece of news. His wife Elizabeth is with child!

Zacharias, even though hearing this straight from an angel's mouth, is absolutely dumbfounded. "How can this be?" he sputters, "seeing as how, um, um, you know?!" Perhaps as punishment, perhaps just to curtail what would surely have been his insufferable braggadocio, Zacharias is informed he has uttered his last words for the duration of Elizabeth's term. He is literally struck dumb. So when cousin Mary arrives, she and Elizabeth can have their visit in peace, compare notes on first-time pregnancy, and generally enjoy each other's company. Mary stays with Elizabeth for three months.

Now when she returns to Nazareth, she has some "splainin'" to do. The virgin Mary is obviously "with child." *Embarazada*, as they say in Spanish. A big embarrassment she is indeed to her future husband. How can she explain? Did she even try to? The biblical account is silent on this.

We do, however, get a picture of Joseph, "a just man." Luke tells us he was "minded to put her away privily." That King James Version language is not an allusion to sticking her in some Hebrew equivalent of a nunnery or sending her off to a home for unwed mothers. No, it meant killing her in a private place—like in the backyard—rather than submit her to a public stoning. We've had ample descriptions of what that entails, even in these modern, supposedly more advanced times. Mary's situation, in that part of the world, in that era, was every bit as dangerous as it would be for her if she were living in Afghanistan or Iran nowadays.

But Joseph was not only "a just man," he was a good listener as well. If he didn't lend an ear to Mary, he had his heart open to something. Was it perhaps to his own conscience? Was it to the voice of God? Could he have heard the same angel Gabriel who had appeared to his young fiancée a few months before? One way or another, Joseph got the message: *This is a "God thing." Don't kill her. Take her to be your wife. Raise the child and call him Jesus.* So he did.

According to Matthew, he "knew her not" until she delivered her child. According to Catholics, he never knew her in the biblical sense. Jesus was her one and only child. She was a virgin forever. Protestants, Bible historians, and many others hold a variety of other views. But however we know her today, Mary matters.

Look up the Hebrew root of her name, and you'll find *marah*. Not only does it mean bitter, but also *to rebel, resist, cause to provoke, be disobedient*. These are pretty contrary characteristics to be attributed to a sweet little virgin, right? They are pretty contrary characteristics to be attributed to anyone, particularly to a woman. But they are oh such essential qualities for anyone who struggles to be the person deep within!

So, here's a question: Does naming a girl "Mary," or a derivative thereof, automatically instill a tendency toward rebellion? Or is it the other way around? Could it be that Mary is a name to be earned? Is it possible that those guys who squatted around the ancient communal fire, or the ones who debated and discoursed in the temples and synagogues, who originally told and retold and finally put down in writing the stories that eventually became "The Bible," might have coined a code word for any rebellious, resistant, disobedient, contrary woman who put forth the effort to be herself? Might they have re-christened those rowdy girls Mary? If that's so, here's a toast to Mary, and to the Virgin in us all. And while we're at it, here's a toast to the Josephs who cherish those Marys, who listen, and love and learn.

María and José—probably the most common names in Mexico. There's a warm welcome waiting for modern day Marys and Josephs as well.

42

ONE MORE MARY

I grew up with a picture of Mary Baker Eddy on the wall of the Sunday school I attended. I thought she went to our church and was my friend's grandmother. Mrs. Twedell had the same fine features, kind eyes, and soft curly hair as those in the picture. When I saw her on Sunday mornings I would greet her with great affection. She was, so I thought, the author of the prayer I said every night:

> Father-Mother God,
> Loving me,—
> Guard me when I sleep;
> Guide my little feet
> Up to Thee.

Now that I'm all grown up, I appreciate Mary Baker Eddy in a whole different way. She was fifty-four years old, both a widow and a divorcee, when she first published the work she is known for today. *Science and Health with Key to the Scriptures* is still in print, one of those perennial classics every author dreams of writing. She was fifty-eight when she founded her church, sixty when she chartered her college, sixty-two when she began her publishing house. Throughout the rest of her life she continued writing and speaking extensively. She also healed.

Her healing work and that of her students gave her credibility in many quarters. It also brought fame—both benign and malevolent. The "media" in America at the turn of the nineteenth century consisted of two major newspaper groups, headed by two powerful and influential men. Because the son of William Randolph Hearst had been healed of polio with Christian Science, the Hearst newspapers treated Eddy kindly. Not so for rival Joseph Pulitzer. Speculative, lurid stories about a woman who was a successful religious leader sold papers. Pulitzer even went so far as to instigate a lawsuit against Eddy on behalf of her heirs, known as "The Next Friends Suit," which questioned her mental capacity to handle her own business and personal affairs. Had she lost this suit, she would have become, in effect, a prisoner in her own home. However, it was quickly resolved in her favor when she had opportunity to speak for herself before a panel of five male "masters," appointed by the court for the purpose of examining her competency. Just and fair men, the panel quickly deemed her fully competent, and the suit was dismissed.

Her response to the whole experience was loving and pragmatic. In her eighty-seventh year she founded *The Christian Science Monitor*, a newspaper whose motto she dictated, and which still appears on the masthead: "To injure no man, but to bless all mankind." *The Christian Science Monitor* is still in publication—and has won numerous Pulitzer Prizes for journalism.

Gillian Gill, one of Mary Baker Eddy's more recent biographers, writes of her a passage that might also be applied to Guadalupe: "She transcends the boundaries not only of her historical period but of the religious movement she founded." Gill continues, "Conventional in her twenties, weak in her thirties, struggling in her forties, a social outcast in her fifties, indefatigably working in her sixties, famous in her seventies, formidable in her eighties, [Eddy] rewrites the female plot and offers new ways to strive and achieve."

Okay, I'm working in my sixties, will happily skip being famous in my seventies, but if I get to my eighties, I intend to be *formidable*. Formidable not like Coatlicue with her snakes and talons, but formidable like Mary Baker Eddy. Perhaps in following that particular Mary's lead, I entered Virgin Territory a long time before I ever moved to Mexico.

CHAPTER 4

THE VIRGIN
ON THE JETTY

Petición para los nabegantes—hijos míos,
bengan a mi en todos sus momentos de afflicciones y yo los protejaré.
Acaso no estoy yo aquí, que soy su madre.

Inscription around the Virgin of Guadalupe
on the jetty at Guayabitos

Before we headed back to California to put a "For Sale" sign on our house and sell most of our earthly possessions, I finally wandered out to the end of the jetty. I wanted to see what that shrine thing was. A well-worn dirt path led along the top of the groin, obviously a high traffic pedestrian way. At the very end, cast in concrete and set on an even higher pile of rocks was the Virgin herself—Our Lady of Guadalupe, *La Morenita, Lupita.*

She was covered in sun-faded plastic flowers, cheap rosaries, candle wax, and pelican poop. There were a number of fresh bouquets as well, mainly roses, offered in mayonnaise jars and plastic water bottles, held in place by ribbons and string draped and crisscrossed around the arms of the large concrete cross that rose behind her sunburst backdrop. Her paint was peeling in some places, freshly patched in others. Maintenance at the ocean's edge is never finished. But it was clear that this was a living shrine, evidence of active faith. I translated the Spanish inscription, mentally correcting the phonetic spelling that substitutes the letter *b* for the letter *v*. *A petition for sailors—My children, come to me in all your moments of affliction and I will protect you. Even though I am not here, I am your mother.*

I've had a long fascination with the Virgin Mary, though through most of my life I've had to keep it pretty quiet. My family is so white, so gringo, and the Virgin is so, well, Catholic.

"It's *art* already," I say to a friend on her first visit to our house in Guayabitos, she of the raised eyebrow, turning to me slowly after spying the ceramic Virgin embedded in the mustard-colored tiles above my kitchen sink. Wait *till she sees the one over the sink in the hallway alcove*, I think. That was a find, a wooden *retablo* three feet high in full color. I've installed it in the niche near the cupola, complete with a row of *votarios*. I am a convert, if not to Catholicism, at least and at last to "Our Lady." It wasn't always so.

I was very young in an America that had not yet elected John F. Kennedy. Candles, flowers, dimmed lighting, exuberant colors, pictures of women with crowns—all were "not our kind of thing." White Anglo-Catholics in mid-twentieth century Lubbock, Texas, were few and far between. They were not as scarce as Christian Scientists. Or Jews. So of course my two best friends were named Janie Ginsberg and Mary Theresa Moore. Throughout my school years, I usually found myself in an ecumenical clique of religious outcasts.

But Virgin or no Virgin, I loved the name Mary. It was always mine if I pretended to be a princess or a queen. I loved the María song from *West Side Story,* and the other Maria song from The Sound of Music. I agreed wholeheartedly with yet another song: it was a "grand old name."

But, the *Virgin* Mary? I just didn't get her. Where did she fit in the whole scheme of things? Sure, she was Mommy in every nativity scene, and there was the "virgin birth" and all. But after the Christmas carols were done for the year, I didn't see what her function was. Christianity seemed to be pretty much the story of a guy. A guy and his guy friends. A guy who was the son of a God who was mostly called "Father," and even though the first-ever prayer I learned started out "Father-Mother God / Loving me," religion on the whole seemed pretty much a guy sort of thing. Except for Catholics. They had Mary. The Virgin. Whatever that meant.

"We don't worship Mary," my Catholic friends would insist, with the same vehemence that I'd insist that my crowd didn't worship Mary Baker Eddy. That name—Mary—seemed to get around. "But," they'd acknowledge, "it's okay to ask Mary to ask God for something you want. After all, God is her son."

I looked at one clover leaf after another with Mary Theresa and her Catholic successors in my acquaintance, all of them explaining to me the Holy Trinity: Father, Son, Holy Ghost. Where did Mary fit in? She didn't even have a leaf on the stupid clover! Except maybe on a four-leaf clover? Was that why they were so special?

"So you ask Mary to ask God for what you want? Then what are the priests for?" I'd ask. "You ask a priest, and the priest asks God. Isn't that a priest's job? Doesn't that make Mary a sort of female priest?"

My friends would look aghast. "Women can't be priests!" they'd say. End of discussion. And yes, I was asking these questions long before I knew what it meant to be a "virgin."

I kept asking these questions because I wanted to know. You see, I'd been to the shrine in Mexico City built in her honor. The experience marked me for life. I had seen Mary in her incarnation as the Virgin of Guadalupe. I had caught a glimpse of the influence she wielded. I had been repelled and fascinated, all at the same time. Who was that woman?

It was 1958, the summer before I entered fourth grade. I went with my dad, my mom, and my little sister Emily, three years my junior, on a June vacation to the Mexican capital. Emily and I had new dresses for the occasion, our first trip on an airplane. The dresses were matching blue with full skirts, and each of us wore a stiff petticoat and white anklets. My mother also dressed up, with her nylon seams straight and wearing lots of Revlon's Love That Red lipstick. Riding on airplanes then was a big deal. You dressed for style, not for comfort. Frequent flyer programs hadn't been invented, because there were no frequent flyers.

We boarded a propeller plane with Pan Am written on the side at the Lubbock Municipal Airport, arriving in true Jackson family tradition at the very last minute. The skycap handed my dad claim checks for our luggage just outside the cyclone fence that separated those who were staying from those who were going. The stewardess—and that's what they were called back then—waited at the foot of the stairway as we hurried across the tarmac and up onto the plane. It was a two-hour flight to San Antonio. I chewed dutifully on a stick of Doublemint gum to keep my ears from clogging up.

In San Antonio we had a layover. At that time, you couldn't go to Mexico without a battery of vaccinations. We may as well have been traveling to darkest Africa. It was up to the medical inspector and customs agent in San Antonio to make sure that all our papers were in order, and they wielded their stamps with an official vigor that impressed upon us the gravity of what we were about. We were going to a foreign country. It was another six hours to Mexico City.

The four of us shared a "special compartment" right behind the flight deck with four airline stewardesses on vacation. I don't think it was first class, but a cargo hold that had been converted to hold more passengers. The primary thing it lacked was air circulation. The seats, four on each side of the aisle, faced each other, so Emily and I were face-to-face with Mom and Dad. But what I was most interested in were the four glamorous women in the seats across the aisle. Intent on making the most of Mexico, they bandied handy phrases back and forth out of a Berlitz *Spanish for Travelers* book. I wanted to learn Spanish, too. I wanted to say bright intelligent things to the people we were going to meet. I wanted to understand what they said back to me. I also wanted to wear high heels, cross my legs, hold a glass aloft, and *clink* the ice cubes.

But I didn't want to smoke. How those women smoked! The air became heavy and hazy with the lazy circles they blew toward the low level ceiling. As soon as one would go out, another would light up. Our new dresses reeked of burned tobacco.

It never occurred to any of us to say anything. It just wasn't done. So I held my head in Mommy's lap and tried desperately not to get sick. But the first thing I did when we entered the air terminal in the capital was get down on my hands and knees and throw up all over the terrazzo floor. *Bienvenido a México!*

We were going to Mexico City mainly for Daddy to meet a business associate. Julio Kahn was an import agent for a number of items manufactured in Germany. The one my father bought from him and resold to his cotton gin customers was an electronic instrument called a Moisture Meter. It had a long metal probe that could be inserted in a bale of cotton, and the analog dial would register the level of water in the cotton— important to know when you're buying or selling by weight. Julio and his wife Emmy were Jewish and lived in Polanco, that area of the Federal District that was home to so many who had been forced to leave Europe not even two decades before. Solemnly, my mother told my sister and me the history of our soon-to-be hosts. Julio had been sent to a concentration camp, and Emmy had smuggled rotten grapes through the fence to keep him alive. When they were given twenty-four hours to get out of Germany, they left, taking their son and daughter with them. Mexico City opened its arms. They came—and they prospered.

My parents were the same age as Julio and Emmy's children. Their son Max and his family lived only a few blocks away, still in Polanco. They had two daughters a little older than Emily and me. My sister and I would stay with the elder Kahns—we were to call them Jimamá and Jipapá, just as their own grandchildren did—while Mom and Dad would enjoy what amounted to a second honeymoon. They checked into the Hotel Del Prado

50

across from the Alameda Park, near to the city's center, and Emily and I got to look around before being exiled to Polanco. The hotel was noted for its elegance and the grand scale of the Diego Rivera mural across one entire wall of the dining room. For some reason it was a big deal that people could just walk in and see it. Evidently it had been hidden for a long time. Why? It looked like a lot of people in crazy costumes all crowded together. The craziest costume of all was a great big skeleton, right in the middle, dressed up like an elegant lady! The mural didn't hold that much interest for either my sister or me. Emily and I happily moved into a glorious week in the more child-friendly atmosphere of *la casa de Jimamá y Jipapá.*

I didn't know then that for nine years the mural, *Dream of a Sunday Afternoon on the Central Alameda,* one of Rivera's most famous, had been hidden from public view, because Rivera had worked into the crowd scene the slogan "God does not exist." Only a year earlier had Rivera reconciled his differences with the Catholic Church and painted over the offending words. Rivera had died six months before our visit in November, 1957.

Polanco in the 1950s had large houses surrounded with lush gardens. It was quiet and safe, though a maid always accompanied us when we walked from Casa Kahn the elder to Casa Kahn the younger. In Lubbock the architecture of the houses we walked by would have been described as Spanish Colonial. *California* Colonial was what our new friends here in Mexico called it. The air was clear and cool in the June mornings, cleansed by the showers that sprang from the sky each afternoon at four o'clock. Crushing the fallen leaves along the sidewalks, I discovered that pepper trees actually smelled like pepper! On the upstairs balcony each morning we ate breakfasts of freshly baked, crusty *bolillos* and hot chocolate. The hot milk was made palatable by stirring powdered cocoa and granulated sugar into it, a ritual to which we gave our full attention. Most exquisite, we learned about mangoes, a taste I would delight in describing for years to come.

With a texture like peaches and a sweet-tart bite that raced to a place somewhere just behind my eyeballs, mangoes have an unwieldy shape with a long flat seed inside. Mexicans refer to this as the *hueso*, a bone, rather than *semilla*, the word used for smaller fruit pits. Jimamá had special silver forks, completely flat rather than arched, which were designed specifically for spearing the mango *hueso* lengthwise. Then cultured and polite people could hold the fruit steady on a china plate and pare away first the peel and then the flesh with a sharp knife. I preferred the way the gardeners ate them, slicing away one side and turning the peel inside out, exposing the flesh to bare teeth and licking the juice off my lips before it ran down my chin. But some behavior ceases to be charming when one reaches the advanced age of eight.

From the balcony we could see over the trees in the garden out across the roof-tops to two snow-covered volcanoes, classical cone shaped Popocatepetl, and the longer lower mountain that resembled a reclining woman, Ixtaccihuatl. Jimamá had steeped herself in the language, legends, and folklore of her adopted country, and she told us the story of the Aztec brave Popo who kept watch over his sleeping lover Ixti. It was Jimamá, a German Jewish immigrant speaking in English, who first told me the story of Juan Diego, the Indian farmer to whom the Virgin Mary appeared on a hill just outside of the city we were visiting. Jimamá gave her version the symmetry you would expect of a native-born German, and the pathos of one familiar with a conqueror's boot.

"There was no 'city' at that time," she explained, "not like the large metropolis of two million we live in now." Jimamá settled into the telling. The great race of Aztecs had fallen to the Spanish barely a generation prior. They were poor and ill-treated, and Juan Diego, an Indian farmer, held his woven *tilma* close about him against the cold of mid-December. But the light of the Virgin, when she appeared to him there in his field on the hill, warmed him all through.

"Build me a shrine," she requested of him. "Go to the bishop, and make my wishes known."

Frightened, but obedient, Juan Diego went to the bishop, who informed him that the Virgin could not possibly have appeared to such a poor miserable creature as an Indian, and she certainly wouldn't make her wishes known in *nahuatl*, the indigenous language. "Go back to your field," the bishop told Juan Diego. "Quit telling lies about the Virgin."

Again she appeared, repeated her request, and again Juan Diego was sent away from the bishop. "How can I know that what you say is true," the bishop demanded, "unless you show me some proof?"

On her third appearance the Virgin told Juan to climb to the top of the hill and look on the other side. There he found a field of red roses, all in full bloom in the cold winter air. Removing his cloak, his tilma, he gathered a huge bouquet of them, wrapping them safely in the folds to carry back to the bishop.

"I have proof," he said triumphantly, unfurling the tilma before the prelate's feet. The roses tumbled out onto the floor. But that was not all! Emblazoned across the cloth of the farmer's cloak was the image of the Virgin. Her hands were folded in prayer, her eyes lowered, her head slightly to one side. She wore a star-covered cloak, and a blaze of sunrays emanated from behind her. Her feet were hidden in the folds of her rose-colored robe, but beneath them a small male angel held a crescent moon on his shoulders. Her robe was belted high above the waist, and she was obviously "with child." Around her was circled a wreath of red roses.

"It is this very cloak which hangs in the Shrine of the Virgin of Guadalupe. People come from all over Mexico to touch it and be healed. We will go to the shrine," Jimamá promised. "Then you'll see. From all over Mexico they come to her. Some on their knees, all the way! Can you imagine?"

No, I couldn't imagine, not at that time.

The elder Kahns had a driver. Through the week or more we were in Mexico City, Eduardo drove Jimamá, my mother, my sister, and me on sightseeing tours in and around the capital, jumping out to open doors on our arrival, snapping them open once more when we returned.

In his care we trooped through Chapultepec Castle. I gazed at the ceiling mural where was painted the image of a boy not much older than I was, throwing himself earthward wrapped in the flag of Mexico. Cadets at the military school housed in the castle had defended it from invading forces in 1847.

"They were fighting Americans," said Jimamá, pointing out the tattered image of the Stars and Stripes in the background of the painting that stretched above our heads.

"We were the enemy?" I asked. The possibility disturbed me.

Inside the castle there were full-length portraits of Emperor Maximilian and his young bride Carlota. How they had expected Mexico to welcome them with open arms! How seriously disillusioned they were! I looked deep in the faces of the haughty figures in their finery. Did they have a clue of the fate before them, a firing squad for Maximilian, and an asylum for Carlota? *At least they weren't Americans,* I thought.

In Xochimilco I dragged my hands in the water, catching the lilies that floated among the pretty flowered boats. Eduardo would hold the buds for me, and I would pinch them with my fingers so they opened with a resounding "pop."

In Coyoacán we stood outside of "some artist's house," as my mother explained, "I think it's the same man who painted the mural at the hotel." I remember it as being blue, and I wished I could see inside. I still haven't ever visited the family home of Frida Kahlo, shared at times with her husband Diego Rivera.

At the Palacio de Bellas Artes we oooh-ed at the Tiffany glass curtain with the images of Popo and Ixti, the two volcanoes we now knew so well. Their images shimmered in the soft theater lights. At night the Zócalo outside lit up like fairyland. Here was the heart of Mexico, the very center of the country with which I knew I was falling in love.

Our visit to the Shrine of the Virgin of Guadalupe came on our last day in the capital. We arrived on the outskirts of the vast paved apron surrounding the shrine, awe-inspiring even at a distance. The building was on a definite slant, which made me want to lean to one side. Jimamá had told the truth. There were kneeling pilgrims, hundreds of them, making their way slowly and solemnly, knee by knee, toward the tilting structure before us.

Many of the women were dressed in loosely fitting overdresses of a sober brown color, such as the cook at the younger Kahn house wore. I had asked her about it. *"Es una promesa,"* she explained, and I was no more the wiser.

"She has to wear it for a year," the younger Kahn girl explained. "Her daughter was sick, and the Virgin made her well."

I still didn't get it. Did the Virgin make deals?

Now I watched, as the mass of pilgrims became individuals. I wondered what their stories were, who had suffered tragedy, who had been healed, who was asking for healing. Close by, two women, wobbly with exhaustion, shared a scarf to cover their heads. Women were not allowed in the shrine without headgear of some kind. My mother looked at Jimamá, the Jew and the Christian Scientist both realizing at the same moment what had been forgotten. None of us had either hats or headscarves!

Ah, but Eduardo had come prepared. From the inside of his jacket pocket he pulled snowy white squares, immaculate and massive *pañuelos*. Handkerchiefs firmly in place on the crowns of our heads, we were ready to join the crowd.

A crowd it was indeed. I clutched the hankie to my head and grasped my little sister's hand with the other. She in turn had tight hold of Mother. None of us were prepared for the mass of crushing, pushing humanity that grew thicker and more agitated as we neared and then entered the shrine itself.

Inside we were part of one great body with myriad hands and faces, moving inexorably toward the *tilma,* the Indian mantle of Juan Diego, preserved for centuries for the benefit of believers. The air was heavy with the scent of flowers and burning candles.

We passed by what looked like our babysitter's bulletin board. But these weren't football programs and corsages. They were letters and pictures, handwritten and drawn, describing dire circumstances from which the Virgin had saved the supplicants. There were banks of roses in various stages of freshness and decay, as well as cast metal mementoes in the form of body parts. It looked as though nothing was ever removed. Layer on layer of paper, metal, and petals had built up over time.

Then, there it was, encased in glass, much smaller and dingier than I had imagined, though the colors of the image itself were brilliant. Surprising, I thought, for being over 400 years old. It was exactly the image Jimamá had described. There was no time to study it in detail, though, even if that were possible. The glass panel protecting it was dark with fingerprints, smudges and smears. There was reaching and stretching from the body of the crowd as it moved steadily onward. There were tear-stained faces turned rapturously upward. There were hands touching the glass and then retracting to pat or wipe the body part that needed healing. There were sobs and shudders, wails of either ecstasy or sorrow. Then with a great sigh, the crowd moved on. In short order we were expelled once more to the sunshine.

I was dumbfounded. Never had I witnessed anything comparable. This was messy prayer, exuberant, emotional, enthusiastic, expectant. Oh, I'd grown up with prayer and it was prayer meant for healing, but it was chaste and proper prayer that was reasonable argument more with myself than with any deity. God was perfect, right? So it was up to me to get my feelings and emotions in line—to calm myself, get transparent, to match that big beige amorphous Being. Because God had to be beige. "You can't go wrong with beige," my mother always said. "Beige is always perfect."

What I'd witnessed in the shrine was definitely not beige. It was wild coloring outside any lines of any coloring book I'd ever seen. I didn't know what to call it. Magic? Chaos? I didn't know what to think. The Virgin, Guadalupe style, was a very scary lady. Little did I know then that my best friendships would always be with strong women. When I found the Virgin fifty years later, poised on the jetty beyond my doorstep, I was ready to make her a friend.

DIA DE LOS MUERTOS
DAY OF THE DEAD

She is Catrina, a cadaver dressed in Edwardian elegance, who beckons with a boney be-jeweled finger. She is an icon of Mexican folklore. I painted one for my friend, to use on the altar he's constructing for Día de los Muertos. Her décolletage exposes no soft breasts but bones, skeletal and definitely revealing. If it weren't for her feather boa, you could see right through her. Catrina is the feminine image that epitomizes the Mexican attitude toward death—fatalism with a dash of humor. "Don't you want to dance with me?" she asks. *No quieres bailar conmigo?*

Growing old is no picnic, but in Mexico being dead is one big fiesta, at least on November 2. El Día de los Muertos is when everyone heads for the cemeteries laden with marigolds and festive, anise-laced *pan de muertos*, moundy loaves of bread baked with knobby globs of dough on top to look like skeleton bones. Picnic baskets are packed with favorite foods of the dearly departed, and it's party time at the *panteón!* It used to really creep me out. I say, used to.

There's something I've grown to like about the idea of honoring someone we've loved who has gone on beyond, giving an annual tip of the hat to the animus that made them unique. "Hank always liked a party," my mother-in-law said dryly, informed by the sales representative at the Neptune Society that my father-in-law's remains would be travelling to the Santa Ana crematorium in the company of six others. It broke the post-mortem sobriety. She, Larry, and his brother broke into peals of laughter remembering the happy spirit Hank always brought to any gathering.

Both Hank and Chloe have gone on to whatever adventures lie beyond the visual range of what Larry and I can see. I find myself lighting candles on Día de Los Muertos, usually the first cool evening of the year here in the Mexican tropics. The memories we have of them are mostly happy. But what is the "spirit" of anyone but our sense of who he or she was? The past is always subject to refining and revision. Keep the good, let the other go. Picnics, pungent marigolds, and *pan de muertos* can only help the process.

I write this and look at the name of the flower. Marigold. Could it be? I google. It's true. "Marigold" is literally Mary's Gold, a type of sunflower associated with the Virgin. What better blossom could there be to give grace to a grave?

CHAPTER 5

THE FIRST CRISIS

I don't care if it's dark and scary, long's I got my Virgin Mary,
riding on the dashboard of my car.
Gold Coast Singers

The house on Golondrinas welcomed us with open arms. So did the neighbors. The gringos of the Zona Residencial are a friendly lot. But by the time we were "officially" moving in, I was barely able to move, let alone stand and welcome Mona, who came bearing a huge Talavera compote filled with fresh fruit, or Ally, the official welcoming arm of the homeowners' association, or Jeanette, who hitched up her *parejo* across an ample bosom and steamed across the street to make my acquaintance. She didn't like what she saw.

"I want you to meet my husband," she said, and charged back across the street. A few moments later, reluctantly following her, came Bruce, retired physician, stethoscope and blood pressure instrument in hand. Not a good sign. He was gentle and rather apologetic, not wishing to intrude. I was wide-eyed and weak. I had no idea what was wrong with me. I just knew I hurt, and had hurt for much too long a time.

The last eight months had passed in a blur, selling, packing, and discarding, sorting through the accumulation of not only our own lives together, but that of my in-laws. Larry's mother had passed on six years before, and we'd never really had time to sort through her household belongings. They'd been stored in our attic, waiting distribution to family back in Texas. "Come *now*," we directed his brother and children. "If you want anything at all, this is the time to claim it." So they came, along with a solid cavalcade of houseguests getting their last chance at free lodging near the beach in South Orange County.

There was also a constant procession of strangers passing through, as we seemed to be in the middle of a perpetual garage sale. I didn't bargain. I practically gave things away. My body felt like it was sinking, and in desperation, as if I could lighten the weight I felt in my chest, I began jettisoning all but that which I deemed most essential. My library was essential, I knew, but fighting for every breath, I didn't have the strength to decide which books to leave. I brought them all, forty cartons worth, which now lined one side of the hallway leading to the verandah.

And there was my office. Closing it and saying goodbye to the other five women who staffed it through the week was heart wrenching. For almost four years our unified Safe Harbor Healing had provided a refuge and resource center for those looking for healing of spirit, mind, or body. Most of the clientele were women. It was a small consulting office that provided privacy for those seeking help—a place to mentally drop anchor. Located close to the Dana Point Marina, the name had been an inspiration that came during one of my morning walks around the harbor.

But it had been a long time since I'd taken one of those walks. For the past year or more it was all I could do to get out of bed. The healing counsel and help I provided others didn't seem to be working for me. I was confused and resentful. Under it all there was a deep-seated anger. I didn't want to talk about it. Didn't want to deal with it. I just wanted to get away. I was running to Mexico as fast as I could. Now in Mexico, I wasn't any better.

That didn't stop me from coming up with a defensive spiel to greet the ministrations of my new neighbor as I acquiesced to the stethoscope, to the pumped up band around my arm, and Dr. Bruce squinting at the gauge. Normal. But I obviously wasn't healthy. I could barely breathe.

"You might want to have a blood test some time pretty soon," he suggested gently. I thanked him, told him I'd think about it. The last thing I wanted was a needle in my arm.

A few days later I wanted *something*. Anything. Also, I was facing Larry's stark fear. "Don't you dare die on me and leave me here alone," he said through gritted teeth. "I don't speak Spanish."

Who was I kidding? Myself. For three generations Christian Science had been the only, and I mean *only* health care our family had known. We were literally "those people who don't go to doctors." It wasn't as if we'd sailed through life meeting nary an unhealthy bump in the road. Our family road had as many potholes and cobblestones as Calle Golondrinas. Christian Science had been there and brought us through.

The stuff wasn't magic. There was method involved. I knew it worked, just as surely as I knew if I got on an airplane, taxied down the runway at the right speed and lifted the nose, eventually I'd be flying. The problem was, with the condition I was now facing, I hadn't even started my engine. Oh, I'd been going through the motions for some time, mainly for the benefit of friends and family. I'd been sitting with "the books," the Bible and Mary Baker Eddy's *Science and Health*, open on my lap, looking pensively pious and receptive. I might as well have been flapping my arms and making *vroom, vroom* noises. No airplane takes off with a load of ice on its wings, and my mental wings were bound up tight with an icy anger and resentment that had been building up over the last two years.

First of all, I was mad at Bush and his whole administration. Even without all the later revelations of deceit and lies, the whole Iraq scenario and his re-election made me livid. There were not many sympathetic ears at that time in far southern California. San Diego and Orange Counties are two of the most religiously and politically conservative spots in the whole country. "Patriotism" meant not dissenting, and I found myself biting my tongue, my lips, and the insides of my mouth in the face of the gung-ho Bush fever of a large portion of our friends and neighbors.

I couldn't find much comfort in family, either. The second source of anger was a complicated asset protection plan my dad had concocted that bound me and my siblings like four cats with tails tied together and thrown over a clothesline. There were three girls and one brother. Our conversations usually revolved around the business and were fraught with a lot of protracted silences when each of us girls tried to curb our tempers and preserve "family harmony."

Finally, I was mad at my church, the one place I'd always felt I could go to find comfort and understanding. I wasn't taking issue with the basic premises of Christian Science. It was management with whom I had a problem. A new administration was essentially denying the validity of the work I'd been doing for the last ten years, which was introducing Mary Baker Eddy as a voice worthy to be heard on her own, irrespective of the religious culture that had grown up around her. Now, it seemed, a largely male contingent wanted to stuff her back behind the scenes of the very institutions she had founded, emphasizing her "ideas" rather than her life story, as if the two could be separated. Another case, it seemed to me, of "Thanks for the baby, Lady. Now go get lost."

Country, family, and church—I could no longer comfortably identify with any of them. I repeatedly dreamed of being left in the middle of the Pacific watching an ocean liner named "The Mother Ship," sail off into the distance. I watched it go with mixed feelings of relief and anxiety. Who was I if I weren't a loyal American, a member of the Jackson family business, and a "good" Christian Scientist?

I'd grown used to biting my tongue and swallowing words. I retreated into resentful, cynical silence. I didn't want to talk about any of this, *avoided* talking about it, was almost ready to roll over and die rather than deal with it. Then, the doctor I saw at Amerimed Hospital in Puerto Vallarta essentially gave me that choice.

In the early morning hours, a few days after moving into the house on Golondrinas, I asked Larry to take me there. I submitted to a blood test and waited for the results. Dr. Marquez looked serious. "I don't know what you're doing still walking around," he said.

Evidently the blood test showed I didn't have a lot of blood left. My hemoglobin count was 4.2—12 to 16 is normal. No wonder I'd been scaring small children on the streets. I was bearing a strong resemblance to something like a real live Catrina, that skeletal folklore image of Death.

Several days and four units of whole blood later, plus a lot of hours in an operating room with the surgeons trying to find the source of the blood loss, I thought I was good to go. Silly, state-of-denial me. The blood loss had been gradual but constant. It had been going on for the past two years. "Hemorrhoids," I self-diagnosed. "It will all be fine when I stop this crazy schedule, quit sitting on airplanes, and finally get some exercise."

So I walked the beach and tried to get up from the computer screen, but the blood loss continued. Four more times over the next year and a half I'd return to the hospital. In total I depleted the Puerto Vallarta blood bank by twelve units. There were colonoscopies, barium enemas, tests, pokings, proddings, scannings. Medical conclusion: I had a perfectly healthy body except for diverticulitis and some hemorrhoids. "Watch what you eat. Avoid salsas and seeds." There was no other physical reason, they said, for my continued bleeding and weakness.

Where modern medicine left off, my Mexican friends stepped in. There was no end of folkloric remedies offered by Chano, by Hilda, by Jeanette's housekeeper María, by anyone who knew that *la güera*, the white woman, was suffering. Every week I was offered leaves, bark, viscous lumps of vegetation, all with detailed instructions for making *infusiones* to be taken slowly before bed or first thing in the morning or five times a day, or sometimes under a new moon. There were pomades made from rattlesnake oil, from peyote, from placentas of who knows what. There were milled seeds and flours, flower petals and Flor de Bach, the essence of *pasiflora* that was to relieve the dark spot of tension "there, *Señora*," the Rieki massage therapist, semi-chiropractor *curandera* I was seeing diagnosed. "There, *Señora*," she emphasized, touching me between my breasts. "There in the core of your being; you have a great pain in your heart."

Well, no joke. The problem was, what was I going to do about it?

THE HEART OF THE HOUSE

The heart of our house was empty. Jim and Janet wanted us to buy their furnishings, but as we say in West Texas when confronted with sellers' optimistic price tags, "They were real proud of that dining room table." The cupola room stood empty, a swollen nodule on the passage from the front door to the back. Only our back passageway was practically impassable, lined as it was with cartons of books. The first order of business was lining the rotunda with built-in bookshelves that would curve around one half of the room.

The work commenced the first of November, at six a.m. sharp. Sharp, as in "chink, chink, chink." I got used to waking to the sounds of masonry, once Larry let the workers in. The bookshelves were massive, poured concrete that began at floor level and proceeded upward, each two-inch thick shelf supported by those below it and sapling trunks cut to the height I desired for each level. No worry about these shelves sagging under the weight of my body of literature. Each could support the weight of several men. We were building a fortress. At last the gray cement was plastered and painted, and topped with ceramic tiles. The bookshelves were there to stay a long, long time.

So were we, I decided, and asked that the tile my mother-in-law had carried back from Italy be embedded on one of the support columns. It was an image of St. Francis of Assisi. Javier the painter was intrigued. Gringos aren't usually religious. Would I be interested in the Festival of the Virgin? It was to begin the next day, December 11.

CHAPTER 6

CHRISTMAS
IT STARTS WITH THE VIRGIN

I love to observe Christmas in quietude, humility, benevolence, charity ...
Mary Baker Eddy

Do not plan on getting anything done in Mexico between December eleventh and January sixth. The Christmas Season is celebrated with intensity and fervor in Mexico, but it is far from the commercial venture that in the States starts when Halloween candy is cleared from the shelves, and dribbles on into January with 75% mark down sales. Such is not the case south of the border. Christmas celebrations start December 11, and end the night of Epiphany, January 6, after which nary a loaf of Three Kings bread can be found. They're *gone,* not sitting out on some half-price day-old shelf. When the party's over, it's over. But while it lasts, it is wholehearted.

I like that kind of observance—a definitive sort of celebration that says *this* day is a really big deal. Growing up, I was always vaguely disappointed in Christmas Eve. I knew about the real meaning of Christmas, the spirit and everything—the joy of giving, communicating with family and friends, peace on earth, feeling the warmth, ho, ho, ho. I'm talking in particular about the six hours on Christmas Eve, right after supper through midnight. It seemed to me that there should have been something spectacular about that particular time span, but it never really happened.

We were an informal sort of family, more inclined to playing Parcheesi on Christmas Eve than doing something "special." Oblivious of the fact that playing board games in a safe household warmed by central heating with a full refrigerator and pantry and closets full of adequate winter clothing would be considered pretty "special" in most parts of the world, I longed for more.

Specifically, I wanted dim lights, candles, music, choral singing, angels, hallelujahs, cherubim, seraphim, and awe-inspiring mystery. I wanted animals singing at midnight, rings around the moon, cosmic phenomena, and a few pyrotechnics for good measure.

"Turn on the TV," Mom would say. "Doesn't Perry Como or Andy Williams have a special on tonight?"

As I matured—well, as I grew to the age that I could drive a car—I broadened my search for the perfect Christmas. I attended my friends' parents' cocktail parties and drank ginger ale from crystal stemware. It felt glamorous with all the sparkly, slinky dresses and laughing crowds. But that still wasn't it. Too much cigarette smoke. I wanted candles, darn it, not tobacco.

I explored Christmas Eve services with my friends. Catholics and Episcopalians had the dimmest lights and the tallest tapers. Still, I never quite found that magic thrill in the tummy.

Returning home, I'd find Mom finishing off in the kitchen. "Have a good time, dear?" Dad would look up from *The Wall Street Journal*. "Have you been somewhere?" I'd sigh and retire to my bedroom, light a stumpy little votive candle, and listen to "The Nutcracker Suite" in the dark. There just seemed to be a hole where Christmas Eve should be.

Larry's family had a little more tradition. They sat around the fireplace each Christmas Eve after dinner, and my mother-in-law-to-be, Chloe, would read *How the Grinch Stole Christmas*. Not exactly Dickensian, but at least they had a focus.

"We hated it," confided Larry.

"Big time," agreed his brother.

I confided my Christmas Eve longings to Chloe. As mothers-in-law go, I had hit the jackpot. Chloe thought I was wonderful, and I blossomed in her presence. She also understood my longing for mystery, being a candle/dim lights sort of person herself. So one year she bought three tickets to *The Glory of Christmas,* the over-the-top production put on annually by Robert Schuller's Crystal Cathedral. Live camels in church, angels swinging from the rafters, choral selections that made those rafters ring. Sheer entertainment, sort of a Christian Cirque de Soleil—enjoyable, but, we all agreed, not something we wanted to make a tradition.

I eventually gave up Christmas Eve expectations and settled into loving a quiet holiday alone with Larry and whatever furry creatures were currently in residence. We'd exchange small gifts, and make sure Rascal, or Britta, or Velcro the Cat had something tasty in the kibble bowl. We agreed. Christmas Eves like that were pretty special.

But now, Mexico had a gift for me, the fulfillment of a childhood dream.

It was Chano and Hilda who invited me to join them the evening of December 11, the first year we arrived. I was ready for an adventure. Chano was a member of a dance troupe, engaged to perform at a small church in the hills up behind La Peñita in celebration of the Virgin. Dancing, music, candles, fireworks at two a.m.—all would be part of this night of the *velada*, watching with the Virgin until the break of dawn.

"Why all night long?" I asked.

"She is with us all the time," Hilda explained to me. "Watching with her one night without sleep is our *ofrenda.*"

My friend Jeanie was interested in local color, as well. We accepted. Chano beamed. *"Perfecto!"* he exclaimed. He and Hilda and her son Chuy would come by for us at seven that evening. By the way, would we mind driving?

They came elegantly dressed, Chano in a white *guayabira* shirt, black trousers, and suede cowboy boots, Hilda with her hair down, lipstick and eye shadow carefully applied, and a silky red rose tucked behind her ear. Their attire was spotless, despite the fact they had come several miles from their home in La Colonia walking and then in a "combi," rural Mexico's version of mass transportation. We piled into Jeanie's SUV. We crossed Highway 200, and left behind the tasteful and restrained white palaces of ocean-side gringo gulch. We plunged into a labyrinth of dirt streets and brilliantly painted square boxes, lavishly lit with twinkling color and crepe paper streamers. We drove through festive color for what seemed forever. Chano ceaselessly urged us on, *cortito mas adelante*—a little bit further.

But there was no dance that night. The chief musician had fallen ill earlier that evening and was taken to the hospital. Panel trucks and taxis had brought people from as far as twenty miles away, but there was to be no fiesta.

"Would you like to go to a mass instead," asked Chano, "in a little church, *cortita distancia* away?"

"Oh, why not?" we responded. We were dressed up and ready for folklore. We might as well go someplace.

Back behind the wheel we wandered dirt lanes and dry stream beds until we came on the makeshift structure that served a small congregation. There was a concrete floor and two block walls supporting a palm palapa, the whole structure obviously a work in progress. On one of the solid walls was the altar and image of the Virgin. Around her there were layers of filmy drapery and strings of blinking, running, and fade in/ fade out Christmas lights, and flowers, at least four enormous formal arrangements of carnations, gerbera, and tuberose. But most magnificently, cascade after cascade of roses and roses and roses—all of them red, the "sign" given to Juan Diego as proof of the Virgin's appearance.

There was no priest, and there were only women in the congregation—except for Chano, Hilda's twelve-year-old son, and one very old man in a wheelchair. We were provided plastic chairs, which, like the congregation around us, were of varied age, physical condition, and color. Jeanie and I were offered nice white new ones. We demurred, but no, no, we were *bienvenidas*—welcome. Welcome and honored.

We sat down to hear the end of a homily. It was delivered by a woman. She spoke of how prayer isn't something we just offer in church, it's what we do every moment of every day, in our kitchens, caring for children, walking down the street. She said that it doesn't require great education to commune with the divine, that the Indian Juan Diego was proof that God spoke to humble, receptive hearts, and that we should look for the sacred in every place we find ourselves.

Then she asked us to stand as she introduced the rosary portion of the service, telling us that as we went through the prayer, every "Santa María" was a rose to honor the Virgin, and that there couldn't be enough roses to honor her.

"This is going to take a while," Jeanie whispered to me under her breath. "The mother of my daughter's dad was Catholic."

It took a moment for me to figure that out. Finally: "Your ex-mother-in-law?"

"Yeah," she replied. "I guess that's one way to put it."

Does the word rosary come from "roses"? There were many that night. On and on and on went the "Santa María"s. I counted at least six repetitions of the Lord's Prayer, *El Padre Nuestro,* which comes at the end of each round. Now, I know those words in Spanish, but there was no way they could come out of my mouth as fast as they tumbled through this congregation. Each time it was said, I looked up expectantly, thinking, "This is a good place to end." It didn't. More roses. More Santa Marías. My back ached from standing and looking respectful. I started to see why some people might have "issues" with this church.

But at last it did come to an end, and a voice was raised. "Can we take the children home before the padre arrives and the mass begins?" Jeanie and I looked at each other. That wasn't the mass? Exit! Now! Now! We bowed and thanked our way out.

Out of earshot of the church behind us, Chano had a further proposal: "Would you like to go to a *velada? Cortita distancia.*"

"Is it in a church?" I asked. My respectful demeanor was wearing a little thin.

"Oh, no. It's in a house near the house of my cousin, *una cortita distancia,* just a short distance." He looked pleading, his eyes cutting over to the SUV. There would be hot chocolate, he added, *con canela.* Who can resist a grown man wheedling for cinnamon-laced cocoa? The thought of indulging in a *northern* Northern Hemisphere late night custom here in the tropics, where only weeks before I'd been sweating in front of a floor fan and now was shivering and wishing for a sweater, was tempting indeed. Jeanie jangled the keys, and we were off once more.

The shrine set up at the end of the street where Chano's cousin Luisa lived was alive with candle flames and twinkling lights. We saw it from a distance of about forty yards, where we parked and ducked into a little corner grocery store. The main thing they were selling that evening were *velas,* the white candles poured inside jars with the image of the Virgin on the side.

"A good souvenir," I said to Hilda, indicating my purchase as we made our way down the street. It was transformed for this evening into a green corridor by giant palm leaves arching overhead.

She looked shocked. "It is for the Virgin! You can't carry it away! You must leave it with the others."

She nodded to where we were headed. This altar honoring the Virgin was about twelve feet tall and half again as wide, much larger than the one we had just left at the two-sided church. These banks of flowers formed a wall around the image of the Virgin, every color of rose in the rosy spectrum. They were lit from below by the velas brought by the guests attending. There must have been over a hundred of those guests, all attired in their Sunday best, the children well behaved and sitting quietly on row upon row of those white plastic chairs with which China has blessed the world.

That's what you do at a *velada*—sit quietly and keep watch. Ah yes, and eat and drink. I was handed a styrofoam plate with two tamales and a styrofoam cup filled with hot chocolate. I balanced the plate on my knee and sipped from the cup. Heaven! No ordinary thin milky cocoa this. It was *atole*—made with the same *masa de maiz* used to form tamales. It is liquid, but barely. Thinned slightly with milk, it was heavy with chocolate, ground almonds, cinnamon sticks, and sugar. A cup of this would last a long, long time. I cupped it in my hands, breathed in the aroma, and looked around me. This was magic. Or was it reverence? Maybe that was the missing ingredient of all those past Christmas Eves. Just a quiet space to acknowledge and contemplate a miracle in the company of those we love.

So we kept our vigil, laughing quietly with the children who came up to shyly practice their English, nodding, greeting, shaking hands, and exchanging pleasantries with a myriad of Chano's relatives. Eventually, our hands grew heavy and our eyes glazed over. I longed for bed and a chance to sleep off the chocolate and tamales. If Mexico has "comfort foods," I nominate those. Chano and Hilda were gracious, assuring us that they were now close to home. They could find a ride. Jeanie and I were free to go. It was long after midnight, and we excused ourselves.

But sleep was not an option that night. I was safe at home, but the festivities of the *veladas* continued through the night hours. The decibel level spanned a wide range, from the soft singing of those huddled around a fire on the beach not far from our front door, to the window-shaking explosions of *pyrotécnicos* every hour on the hour. At three o'clock Julio Preciado and his entourage struck up an exuberant concert that sounded like it was located on the verandah behind us rather than half a mile away. Our current keeshond, Cody, spent the night panting, barking, and drinking vast amounts of water.

It was dawn when the music stopped, the strains of *Las Mañanitas* left hanging in the air. Everything stopped, all the fireworks, singing, the sounds of makeshift instruments and professional ones. Silence descended, broken only by bird song. It was as if the world around us heaved a great sigh and settled into rest. Christmas had begun.

LAS MAÑANITAS

Traditionally sung for birthdays, and particularly
as a serenade to the Virgin of Guadalupe
at 11:00 p.m. on December 11

Estas son las mañanitas
que cantaba el Rey David
Hoy por ser día de tu santo
te las cantamos a ti.

Coro:
Despierta, mi bien, despierta,
mira que ya amaneció
ya los pajarillos cantan,
la luna ya se metió.

These are the morning songs
that King David used to sing.
Because today is your birthday
We are singing them to you.

Chorus:
Awaken, My Dear, awaken
and see that the day has dawned,
now the little birds are singing,
and the moon has set.

CHAPTER 7

THE BACKSIDE OF TEPEYAC

... the symbol of God functions ...
Elizabeth A. Johnson

W e were going to be very late. It was already well after nine o'clock at night, and the streets of Mexico City were still filled with late evening holiday traffic. I'd flown into the Federal District that January afternoon, the day before Three Kings Day. Mexicans everywhere were winding down a long holiday season that had begun almost a month before.

The dregs of the holiday seemed to be swirling down the drain at the very center of the country. Here in the Zócalo at the city center, skaters circled round and round the temporary ice rink that covered half of the square. Around them on the perimeter streets that defined the square, cars moved slowly, taking in the lights, the music, and the general revelry. On one side the National Cathedral towered over the scene, unlit and silent. On the remaining three sides of the square, multi-colored Christmas lights festooned the building facades. At the center, like a giant swizzle stick caught in the swirl surrounding it, rose the multi-storied Christmas tree—according to some, the tallest in the world—in its last day of glory.

But we were headed away from the Zócalo, north on Avenida Insurgentes, our goal a neighborhood nestled against the hill of Tepeyac, up against the shoulder of the Basilica of Guadalupe. There were three of us in a determined little Volkswagen, swimming upstream away from the whirlpool of activity behind us. Traffic was still heavy, even going in our direction. Decisions about which lane to get in and where to turn had to be made well in advance. So we missed the turn to the Basilica. *"A la derecha"*—to the right—is very similar to *Derecho! Derecho!* which means "go straight ahead." Jorge was driving, and though he was *chilango* by birth, a native of Mexico City, thirty-three years of living in San Francisco had clouded his memory of the finer points of taking directions in Spanish from a backseat driver. Wilfrido, his brother, was torn between the roles of being tour guide and being navigator. We were going to meet Wilfrido's friend, who was an expert on the Virgin of Guadalupe.

Jorge had gone straight ahead—*derecho*—when he should have turned right—*a la derecha*. We were now committed to driving completely around the backside of Tepeyac to arrive at the house of Horacio Senties—*much* later than when we were expected, even given the Latin tendency of arriving fashionably past the appointed hour.

Mexican traffic has a lot to do with lack of punctuality. If competitive left-hand turning were an Olympic event, the country of Guadalupe would be able to reclaim much of the gold carried away by its conquerors. *The race is not to the swiftest,* I realized as we crawled northward. The traffic prize—whatever it is, maybe just arriving at all—goes to the most daring and dauntless. We were novices, and cowards, as well as semantically challenged. As a consequence, we were going to be very late.

I had known Jorge for years in the States, but I was just now meeting the part of his family that lived in Mexico. They were an impressive lot, highly educated and erudite. The majority were either university professors or medical professionals. Jorge himself had been a surgeon before he converted to Christian Science. The brother in the back seat was an engineer.

"What street are we on?" I asked.

Wilfrido answered me with a sound like a sneeze.

"Salúd!" I responded, and he had the grace to laugh.

I saw later it was Ehecatepac, a narrow two-lane road that followed the crease where the large Hill of Tepeyac rose out of the surrounding flatland. Had we turned right at any point, the intersecting street would have come to a dead end or climbed upward at a nosebleed angle in a jumble of cobblestones and stairways. I doubted seriously whether the people living in the stacks of houses attached to the hill could possibly have depended on cars to get them home. Cog trains or donkeys would have been more practical.

It was well past ten o'clock when Wilfrido started cautioning, *"Despacio, despacio. A la derecha. Aquí está!"*

Wilfrido's friend, Horacio, elegant and erect with a shock of snow-white hair, was waiting for us outside a nondescript graffiti-covered gate. He signaled a porter to open it and let us in. As so often happens in Latin America, we were admitted to another world, completely different from the one that lay outside along the roadway. Behind us the door closed, and before us was a well maintained, immaculate, bricked courtyard with room for several cars parked at varying angles. We slid into a space and emerged to *abrazos,* explanations and assurances of *no importa, no importa* about how tardy we were. Horacio was going to stay up this late anyway.

We entered a small door and followed Horacio up a narrow black marble staircase that circled up a story or more. Emerging at the top, we saw rooms of a comfortable residence stretching off to the left. But we were led to the right, *a la derecha,* through several rooms that looked like set pieces from museums. I had paused in front of a glass case with a black woolen military jacket, its red inset covered with gold braid.

"It belonged to Morelos," our host explained and moved on.

The name was familiar, and my mind clicked backwards through mental index cards of Mexican heroes. I had to look him up later. José María Morelos was a priest recruited to be a soldier by Father Hidalgo when he raised the banner of the Virgin of Guadalupe and began the Mexican War of Independence in 1810. Morelos was charged with bringing the southern part of the country under control. There is now a state there that bears his name.

And so it went as we passed through several rooms and finally into the reception office of Horacio Senties Rodríguez, a retreat that might have belonged to a Latin American Dumbledore with a penchant for images of popular religiosity. Among the many representations of Guadalupe, the shelves and shelves of gilt-trimmed books, African masks, framed engravings, photographs, and certificates, there was a life-size Jesus on a massive cross, an authentic Egyptian sarcophagus, a Buddha's head, several carved heads of Nefertiti, and an ebony statue of Shiva. From the ceiling hanging from an opulent glass-beaded light fixture, was a large Oaxacan *alijibri* dragon. Unobtrusively displayed on the far wall, modestly but elegantly framed, was a signed citation with a gold medal beneath it.

For Horacio is a recognized expert in the field of Guadalupana. He quickly warmed to his subject when he realized he could speak freely in Spanish and I would understand. Over the next two hours he spun the tale of the research he had followed in establishing the actual existence of Juan Diego and the real role the Indian had played in promulgating the legend of the Virgin of Guadalupe. It was for this research and the resulting canonization of Juan Diego that Horacio had received papal recognition, the gold medal, and gratitude from John Paul II.

"'Did the Virgin really appear to Juan Diego?' is the question everyone asks," Horacio initiated his soliloquy (this is a translation). His answer, spreading his hands and shrugging his shoulders: Probably not. "But that doesn't matter," he assured us. "What matters is that the story was told in the first place. What matters is who told it. What matters is the effect it has had on the history of Mexico and the place of the church in that country. What matters," Horacio emphasized as he wound up his introduction, "is that Juan Diego was real. It is his story that is most important to understand if we are to understand the influence of Guadalupe."

First of all, Juan Diego was not a poor peasant farmer. His genealogy stretches back to the progenitors of the indigenous community on the shores of Lake Texcoco, a husband and wife named Azcaxochitli and Netzahuálpilli. He was in fact, Chichimec royalty. The Chichimec society was suffused with worship of the benevolent earth goddess Tonantzín, and Juan Diego was a direct descendant of Tonantzín's most prominent priest, Netzahualcóyotl. But how was it that a devoted servant of a pagan goddess could become an earthly messenger for such a thoroughly Christian figure as the Virgin Mary?

Because between Tonantzín and Mary, there wasn't that much difference. Tonantzín had appeared in many forms through the ages. Just like Roman gods are layered on top of Greek gods, why wouldn't Tonantzín appear once more in the form of the Virgin as Guadalupe? Besides that, according to some scholars (Horacio tilted his head forward and raised his eyebrows, giving an indication that he counted himself among that "some"), the image of Mary had already arrived on Mexico's shores long before Cortés and his entourage made their appearance.

"Christianity was present in Mexico before the conquerors arrived?" I asked. Now here was an alternative historical account indeed! Horacio settled into telling the story, and I struggled to follow it.

Tradition has it that different apostles were responsible for bringing Christianity to various parts of the world. Peter established the church at Rome, Phillip the one in Ethiopia, James brought Christianity to Spain. According to Mexican tradition, it was Thomas and Luke who arrived in Mexico.

Luke, it seems, was a painter and sculptor, and it is to him the world owes the privilege of knowing what the Virgin Mary looked like. From where exactly this tradition comes is not certain, but evidently it was common "knowledge" in the Renaissance when several artists of the time depicted Luke painting the Virgin Mary's portrait. Evidently he continued his creative efforts on this side of the globe, fashioning a gift for the indigenous converts to Christianity, a statue of the Virgin. What is more, with this particular statue, Luke depicted the Virgin with a dark face to match their own complexions. This, Horacio informed us, was the statue found by Gil Cordero some twelve hundred years later on the banks of the Wadi Lub in Spain.

"Wadi Lub?" I wondered. "Was the origin of Guadalupe's name actually Arabic?"

The Moors ruled Spain for almost 700 years, and I knew the Spanish language is chock-a-block with Arab derivatives. Practically every Spanish word beginning with *al* has its origins with the Moors. Many of these have to do with water: *alberca* (swimming pool), and *aljibe* (water storage tank). Then there is the wistful *ojalá*, which precedes a spoken desire, meaning "if Allah wishes."

Wadi is also an Arabic word that, though it doesn't appear intact in Spanish, has been adopted as a universal geographic term. It refers to those steep-sided washes in the desert that are filled with rushing torrents after rainstorms. Most of the year, the bed of a *wadi* is bone dry, but underground there's water waiting to break through for those who seek it and dig deep enough. Such a stream must have been the Wadi Lub in northwestern Spain. *Lub* is Arabic for "black gravel, black lava, or black stones." It can also simply mean "hidden."

It was along the banks of the Wadi Lub in late thirteenth century Spain that a humble shepherd Gil Cordero tended sheep. There he stumbled upon a statue of a Black Madonna. Perhaps a rainstorm had flushed it out of its hiding place, secreted from the invading Moors who had swept through the Iberian Peninsula some five hundred years before. Slowly the Spaniards were expelling the Moors, and finding such a statue of Mary would have given fresh impetus to what was considered a holy cause. It was reason enough to build a chapel, which grew into a shrine, which eventually became a royal monastery. For four centuries, it was the most important monastery in all of Spain, named for the Virgin who inspired it, Santa Maria de Guadalupe. Christopher Columbus, on his return from the New World he had discovered, made his first pilgrimage to that shrine.

Horacio nodded and smiled, as I was obviously familiar with this part of history. We agreed. How, shall we say, symmetrical that she should appear less than forty years later on the other side of the Atlantic, again to a peasant, again to offer comfort in the face of conquest. Again, a shrine was built.

On how this image of the Virgin that Luke was supposed to have fashioned for the ancient indigenous people of Mexico found its way back to Spain, I was unclear. Horacio explained it in detail, but I was growing fuzzy with the late hour, and his professorial Spanish washed over me like a warm bath. I felt my head drooping.

Horacio was far from finished, however. I revived once more to hear him describe how Luke was not the only one to leave a gift in the New World. His companion Thomas, whose gospel full of feminine images of God would emerge almost nineteen hundred years later in an urn at Nag Hamadi, had gifted the American Indians with his cape, a cape emblazoned with the image of the Virgin Mary. It was, in fact, Horacio maintains, this same image that the Indian artist, Marcos Cepac, had copied onto the *tilma* presented to Archbishop Zumárraga in 1531, as evidence of the Virgin's appearance to Juan Diego. Yes, the very image attributed to a divine hand was actually the work of an Indian craftsman. Did we want to see a copy of the cape of Santo Tomás? Horacio happened to have one. It was hanging in the next room. It was, indeed.

But why would the Chichimecs and their successors have maintained this image of a woman with rays of the sun emanating from behind her, the moon (or a serpent) under her feet, a cloak of stars thrown round her shoulders, and a vessel hanging from the belt around her waist? Could it have been that she fit right in with a pantheon of other feminine images to whom they were already accustomed to paying homage?

The goddess figure, whether she was called Coatlicue or any of her intervening incarnations, had been worshipped on the hill of Tepeyac for centuries. Cihuacoatl, Chicomecoatl, Huixtocihuatl, Xochiquetzatl, and Tonantzín were all feminine deities, earth goddesses all, each known for either a star-studded gown, standing on the moon, a maternity belt, or something that was mirrored in the image of Guadalupe. In order to preserve the cult of the last incarnation, Tonantzín, it would have been expedient for Juan Diego to espouse an image that incorporated combinations from all of them. When asked her name, he supposedly replied, *"Tecuauhtlcupeuh,"* a Nahuatl term meaning, "she who comes flying from the region of light like an eagle of fire," definitely a sign from the Aztec gods.

"Sounds like Guadalupe to us!" responded the Christian Spaniards, thinking of the image found by Gil Cordero and enshrined back home.

Thus both groups, conquering Europeans and conquered Aztecs, could claim the feminine image on Juan Diego's *tilma* as a sign from their deity, could revere her divine origin, and be certain of her purpose for their particular theology. A one-in-herself, one-size-fits-all, honest to whatever-God-you-claim Virgin, enshrined for posterity.

Juan Diego was eventually canonized by the Roman Catholic church on July 31, 2003. It was a victory for the *mestizo* population of Mexico. That he also descended from and perhaps continued the traditions of a high priest of Tonantzín is not, however, mentioned in the official account of the church.

It's hard to kill the goddess. She will "crop up" in many unexpected places, especially if she accompanies the seed in the earth itself. Several years ago I spent a week in Morelia, Mexico, at a language school, just to get the feel of Spanish on my tongue before giving talks in Guadalajara and Mexico City. On my own, I explored the colonial city and its museums. The pre-Columbian displays of tiny terracotta figures held no interest for me at the time. I breezed past the display cases of little fertility goddesses doing—hmmm—fertility things. Evidently the fields around Morelia and throughout Mexico held great numbers of these figures, planted as they were along with the crops.

What I was drawn to was a larger image of herself, Guadalupe, a carefully crafted icon suitable for carrying through the streets on a palanquin on feast days. The attendant explained how the indigenous population had learned new handicrafts through making the Catholic images for the shrines and churches that were being installed all over Mexico. The actual work of manufacturing the images of saints, Jesus, and the Virgin fell in the category of manual labor, no matter how skilled, and was thus consigned to the native artisans.

"Did you see the images in the first room?" the attendant asked. I nodded. I'd seen them. I hadn't given them more than a cursory glance. "Very rough work," he said, *"primitivo."* The Spaniards forbad goddess worship when they came, and ordered all the little idols destroyed. But you know what, *Señora?* There are those in Morelia who still remember when the image of The Virgin fell off the platform when they were carrying her through the streets. She broke, *Señora.* Her backside split completely open. And can you imagine? She was filled with little idols! They were stuffed inside of her!"

THE THINGS WORTH KEEPING

It wasn't just Jim and Janet's stuff in the basement of the house on Golondrinas. Whatever the complicated, true, or untrue version of the history of our house, each owner seemed to have left a little something of themselves in that vast cavern below our main floor. I believe we furnished three or four households in La Colonia, home to Chano and Hilda. They happily hauled out beds and bedding, tables, chairs, sofas, end tables, lamps, and all manner of other treasure.

"*Sí, sirve!*" Chano would assure me, as I looked doubtfully at a termite-riddled table-top or an upholstered cushion grungy with tropical mold. I encouraged the use of face-masks when working below.

But hidden in all the debris were some treasures worth keeping. Stacks of tiles left standing in the crumbles of a cardboard box presented a jigsaw puzzle challenge, revealing a charming Mexican street scene when I finally pieced them together. The tile man engaged to install it on the rounded wall in the cupola pointed out the numbers painted in order on the backs of the tiles. Ahem. Handy, those.

There were tri-fold wooden screens, *divisadoras* Chano called them, ornate and Moorish looking, which Hilda rubbed down with *aceite rojo*, the ubiquitous red oil furniture polish sold in every corner grocery. Made from the *huanacaxtle* wood that was found throughout the rest of the house, the screens were solid and heavy, about seven feet tall. The rich grain of the wood came alive with the polish. Definitely keepers, but I'd have to think just where to use them. I would put them in the cupola, the heart of the house! That's where the treasures seemed to be converging. The heart of the house was coming alive.

CHAPTER 8

WHO ARE YOU, LADY?

And there appeared a great wonder in heaven;
a woman clothed with the sun, and the moon under her feet,
and upon her head a crown of twelve stars.
Revelation 12: 1

While I was culling through the cavernous expanse beneath the house on Golondrinas, I was giving closer examination to my personal theological basement. There was something missing. Country, family, church—I groped my way through the detritus of my life looking for whatever it was I needed to salvage. This was going to take a lot more than a big bottle of *Aceite Rojo.*

By October 2006, the Iraq war of liberation had lost its initial luster, however artificial that luster may have been. I was surrounded in Mexico by snowbird Canadians, who were becoming increasingly unhappy as members of the glorious coalition. I wasn't eager to stand out as a U.S. citizen. When introduced as such, I'd soon be responding to comments regarding "your Mr. Bush," with, "I'm sorry. I'm so, so sorry."

The reaction of relatives to the hospital stays was surprise, dismay, and, from some family members, downright hostility. It didn't help that at the same time I was going through all this, Mom and Dad both experienced health crises as well. When the dust settled, Dad was installed in an Alzheimer's facility, my mother was released from intensive care, and I found myself distanced farther and farther from the family I'd thought I'd known. My sisters were supportive to a certain degree—from a distance and over the phone. But each had families and careers. Dealing with Mom and Dad entailed enough extra travel to put a strain on time and budgets, without adding an ailing older sister into the mix.

It was new friends, strong and capable women, who stepped in to fill the vacuum. I was swept up in a collective love that came from women as distinct and individual as the colors in a *serape*, and as supportive and comforting as an *abuela's rebozo*.

There was Mona who cooked for me daily for two weeks, soft nutritious things that would go through easily after an operation for hemorrhoids. "We'll have you up in no time," she promised. "You'll be doing yoga on our rooftop by Thanksgiving!"

Jeanette and Bruce-of-the-stethoscope from across the street feted my husband on his sixtieth birthday, Jeanette cooking all his favorite American comfort foods from mashed potatoes to white cake with white icing. Ally from down the street had red hair like my sisters, and continually popped in to see if there was anything I needed from town. Susana, from across the vacant lot next door, offered prayers and soft cooing sounds. *"Soy tu tocaya,"* she'd exclaimed when we first met, using the

92

term that identified those with the same first name. It was a comfort just seeing her in the garden in the mornings.

And there was Lucy, a young woman emerging from girlhood who popped into our lives straight out of Oxford. With a degree in English literature in hand, where else would she head but to Mexico? And what other job would she take but as a dancer in the nightly revue at the local all-inclusive resort? "I can't dance at all," she explained, "but I rather think they like the way I look in a costume!"

She did indeed look good. Most twenty-two year old women in rural Mexico have produced at least three children. Lucy, besides being erudite, was lithe, flexible, and extremely lift-able. She joined the dance troop on a whim. "If I'm to be a writer, I must have something to write about!"

She also sounded good. The British pay attention to enunciating vowels, a distinct advantage in speaking Spanish, and Lucy was soon intimately acquainted with a side of Guayabitos to which I would never have been exposed without her company. She brought me flowers and trinkets bought from vendors on the beach and regaled me with tales of night life at Los Cocos that would rival any *telenovela,* the soap operas that unreel their improbable stories over Spanish language television worldwide. Lucy was irresistible, and I was glad when she agreed to move in with us. She brought as much light into our lives as the windows in the cupola.

All these women rallied in a fashion reminiscent of the most ardent "church ladies" of the American Midwest. But as for church itself, there wasn't one close by that I felt even faintly interested in attending. In retrospect, I saw that what

I'd valued most in attending a Sunday service was a sense of community, a place where I could be with people who cared for and about me. But I'd found that community already here in the neighborhood, with no prescribed time schedule telling me when to show up and sing. The sense of camaraderie, gratitude, and rejoicing together was spontaneous and tender. Not a day went by without acknowledgement in some form of the great divine goodness that had brought us all together and held us in such love.

I began contemplating actually living life without a Sunday morning church service. Interesting. Very interesting! When I was a child, church attendance had not been optional. We went. My mother's Southern Baptist roots went deep in Oklahoma topsoil. Her daddy was a deacon, and every moment she wasn't in school or at piano lessons (learning hymns and marching music), she was at church. There was choir practice, Training Union, covered dish dinners, Sunday school, and church service.

And fellowship. Lots and lots of fellowship. "An hour on Sunday and one on Wednesday night is nothing," she'd declare emphatically, detecting even a whiff of reluctance on my part. "Church is where God wants you to be."

So for over half a century, like the Energizer Bunny, I kept going and going and going. Sunday mornings. Wednesday nights. I'd pick up a hymnal full of words I knew by heart, and sing with full-bodied loudness encircled by increasingly dwindling congregations.

Here in Mexico I wasn't singing. Not hymns at any rate. I had discovered karaoke instead. Mexicans were delighted to hear a gringo break into Spanish lyrics, and my riffs on Patsy Cline classics never failed to bring ample applause—maybe because I really was falling to pieces. But in reality when I sang this way, I felt things coming together for the first time in years. A sneaky suspicion began growing on me—maybe God didn't care where or what I sang, so long as I did it with joy.

Another great joy I got living in a beach town was kicking off my shoes and running barefoot in the sand. I soon found myself in a circle of women who were doing just that, denominationally speaking.

There was Melanie, a self-described "warped Catholic," who had traded her Harley for a plot of land in Lo de Marco, a beach town just south of us. She now offered grooming and boarding to pets, and counsel and comfort to their owners.

There was Agneta, descendant of German-speaking Dutch Mennonites who had settled in the 1920s near Chihuahua. A generation later, she had returned to Mexico and was now teaching yoga and holding lunar cycle celebrations.

There was Jane, a former Mormon who had shed her protective garments for a bikini.

There was Nina, daughter of Quakers, who, still treasuring silence and inner light, had painted her walls lavender, sap green, and lemon yellow. She hung an image of Guadalupe by her front door, Tibetan prayer flags from her balcony, and installed a statue of Ganesha in her bedroom.

Then there was me, a lapsed Christian Science healer in and out of the hospital, struggling with questions I'd never dared asked. A new face in a new crowd, I took a cue from my newfound friends and dropped identification with any religious denomination. I wasn't "acting" like a Christian Scientist, anyway. I literally didn't know what to call myself any more.

Indulging my ignorance, I started accepting the occasional glass of white wine, the cold beer on a sunny day. No lightning bolts! No voice from the clouds saying "for shame"! I took two steps forward and started sleeping late on Sunday mornings. I'd have brunch with friends and then go to the beach with the rest of Mexico. On Wednesday nights, rather than going to a weekly Christian Science testimony meeting, I watched the results of *American Idol* in real time. The only thing I was doing religiously was closing my Bible, folding my hands, wiggling my toes in the sand, and lifting my chin to the sun. I was just so tired of Bible lingo and God-talk.

There was one biblical term in particular that had long been rubbing me the wrong way. It had grown from being a minor irritation to a major chafing point, and it was the primary reason for setting my King James Version to one side. It was "the Lord."

It was such a guy way of talking about God. It sounded lugubrious, and each time I heard it, I pictured Reverend Lovejoy in *The Simpsons* endowing the phrase with three syllables: the Lo-erd. I understood its use in the New Testament, when the disciples were talking to or about Jesus. Jesus was a guy, a rabbi, their "Lord." I got that. But it was while listening to or reading the Psalms—those ancient songs of comfort and encouragement that in the past had given me such solace—that I would find myself curbing an urge to throw things against the wall. The Lord this. The Lord that. O Lord! How I groped for a feminine equivalent, just to experiment with how it might feel! "Oh, Lady"? No. Heavens no. That wasn't it at all.

I continued to rebel against I wasn't sure quite what. If someone asked me directly, "What's wrong with you?" I found my jaw clenching and a growl emerging. "I'm pissed off at patriarchy," I'd sneer.

It wasn't exactly a springboard to conversation, and after only a few times I dropped saying it altogether. But really. The language issue seemed to epitomize the whole of my resentment against country, family, and church. Those two words, "the Lord," seemed to render what I held nearest and dearest, my religion, a caustic irritant, not a consolation. Wouldn't it be obvious to someone that this kind of language just didn't fit any more? Was I the only one who felt this way? "Picky and childish, straining at gnats, get a life," I was told in so many words by a variety of Stateside acquaintances when I whined into telephone conversations.

Was I just too far in advance for my old friends? Or maybe I was finally experiencing that event called "consciousness raising" long after many had floated far above me.

I thought back to conversations I'd had with earnest women in coffee houses near college campuses where I was to speak. "Christian Science? You're Christian?" they'd say in the same tone that might have been employed had I announced I still wore granny panties (which I did). "How can you even read the Bible and not get angry?"

To these "post-Christians" and "neo-pagans," my protests about the even-handed way Jesus dealt with both genders, his flouting of religious taboos where women were concerned, and the symmetry of the paired parables in the Gospel of Matthew—one always with a man, the next always with a woman—all these examples fell on deaf ears. As far as they were concerned, Paul had revealed the real agenda of Christianity in his letters to Timothy, Titus, and the Corinthians. Peter's additional two cents worth about the "weaker vessel" had totally tipped the scale away from the feminine side.

Of course, the Hebrew Scriptures were even worse, what with Lot offering up his daughters to a lustful crowd, Jeptheh burning alive his one and only feminine offspring, and any other number of less-than-inspiring ancient Middle-Eastern tribal practices in the pages of Judges, Chronicles, and Kings.

Genesis had a load of good story material—"one long soap opera," a friend observed, listening as I reeled off the history of Abraham through Joseph as a background to problems in the Middle East. It struck me as I told it to her that so many turning points in Bible history were put in motion by women's actions. But then the women just disappeared from the Biblical account as if they'd never been there in the first place, literally written out of the story.

It was Sara who instigated the exile of Hagar and Ishmael, thus assuring another family branch of the children of Abraham. It was Rebecca watering Isaac's camels who caught his eye and later produced the twins Jacob and Esau. Rebecca also perceived that if Esau were entrusted to perpetuate the monotheistic worship of the God who would become known as the God of Israel, the Hebrews would be S.O.L.—so out of luck. Esau was a schmuck. Second son Jacob was no great prize, but he was head and shoulders above his older brother. It was Rebecca who ensured he'd be the progenitor of what became the children of Israel.

Reeling off the tale to my friend in this manner, I grew more and more irritated by the evaporation of feminine images. They seemed as ephemeral as the desert mirages—sparkling and distinct in the distance, and then disappearing entirely when you got close to the story.

But I wasn't ready to write off ages of wisdom literature in the form of the Psalms, Proverbs, and the Prophets. Instinctively I sensed that buried in the patriarchal language there was some quality stuff. But finding it reminded me of the little boy presented with a pile full of manure as a present. Grabbing a shovel with determination, he declares, "There's gotta be a pony in here somewhere!"

Over many years I had collected Bible commentaries, dictionaries, concordances, and translations. In-depth study shed light on many of the stories. As a search and struggle for truth and light, the Bible did present a tale of progress, however excruciatingly glacial that progress seemed to be. But even the most modern translations didn't offer useful feminine terms with which to refer to the divine—alternative terms to which I could relate.

Some translations even made things worse. Eugene Peterson, in the otherwise refreshing *The Message*, repeatedly refers to "God of the Angel Armies," a militant, post-9/11 turn-off for me. So I put the Bible away for a while. I wasn't ready to throw it out entirely, but frankly, I was just tired of the way it sounded.

Then there was its companion in my tradition, *Science and Health. Science and Health with Key to the Scriptures,* to be specific. "They go together," I was always taught, "the door and the key," and Christian Science reading rooms sold them as matching sets, bound in sturdy blue cloth for children, and supple black leather for high school graduations.

But I'd spent the last ten years or so with a tight hold on the "key" part of the duo, *Science and Health.* I had been a member of the official international speakers bureau representing Mary Baker Eddy and her writing, an "expert" on the subject, traveling the world to speak in bookstores, conferences, and classrooms. I had grown familiar with the structure and content of *Science and Health* and also how those had evolved from the time it was first published in 1876 through to 1910, when the author died. Mary Baker Eddy was a constant revisionist, seeming to set as much store by honing and clarifying her concepts as I was now doing to mine. During her lifetime, *Science and Health* went through over four hundred editions.

One of the major revisions Eddy made was just a few years after she first self-published her work in 1876. In the third edition, in a substantial section of *Science and Health,* she used feminine pronouns for God. She continued with that usage over almost ten years, a time when her readership grew exponentially. It was with the fifteenth edition, published in 1886, she reverted to traditional masculine references to God. *Why would she do that?* I wondered with almost a sense of betrayal. She had it so right. Why change it back?

She may have known what Elizabeth Cady Stanton and a cadre of other women (including a former student of Eddy's) had in the works. Irreverent and in your face, *The Woman's Bible* was published in 1896, and throughout its text, it uses exclusively feminine pronouns for Deity. It caused quite a stir at the turn of the last century, as one can well imagine! Then *The Woman's Bible*, relegated to a class of angry feminist literature, sank into obscurity until almost a hundred years later. Did Eddy avoid *Science and Health* being similarly categorized by switching back to the more common usage?

Another possibility that could be considered is that Eddy was so focused on elucidating the broader implications of her ideas, i.e., the ephemeral nature of matter and the healing effect of subordinating the human mind to what she termed the divine Mind, that she didn't wish to distract her readers with what she might have considered secondary themes. Tracking progressive revisions of her work, it is evident that she struggled mightily trying to clarify metaphysical concepts for a public grounded in the physical practicalities of the Industrial Revolution. Why muddy the waters further by bringing up God's gender?

It was familiarity with these previous editions that gave me a broader perspective on her final version of *Science and Health*— broader than what might be gained from a superficial perusal of the current book. What further edits might she have made after 1910, given the changing times and the shifts in political correctness? What wider frames of reference might she have used if she herself had stuck around until after 1975 and Title IX, after so many advances for women—and so many failures? The substance and essential nature of her ideas have certainly stood the test of time; some concepts were so in advance of their time that they have only been recently validated by progress in technology and the advent of quantum physics.

But English is an evolving language, and words set down in 1910 definitely bear the mark of a century that is passed. Given opportunity for further revision, would she perhaps, have given those feminine pronouns another chance?

I rather think she would. In reading through *Science and Health* yet one more time with this gender issue in mind, I began noting in how many instances the author avoided using any pronoun whatsoever when referring to Deity, substituting instead proper nouns, such as Creator, Divinity, Maker, the Great Architect, Origin, Governor, the Eternal Mind, Father, Mother, and the hyphenated and inclusive Father-Mother. Eddy makes extensive use of seven capitalized synonyms for God—Principle, Mind, Soul, Spirit, Life, Truth, and Love— often juxtaposing two or more of them and tossing in an adjective or two—as in "the divine Principle, Love," or "the triune Principle, Life, Truth and Love." All of these allow her to use the neuter-gendered "it" (though referring to God by capitalizing "It" doesn't happen).

But if Muslims have 99 names for God, Eddy uses at least that many in *Science and Health*. With interest I now noted that when she made reference to "the Lord," it was usually when quoting directly from the Bible. This wasn't a term she used readily outside of a biblical context. Did she have as many issues with the term as I did? I wasn't ready to set her or her book aside, even if I did now find myself at odds with the culture that had evolved around her church. One can, after all, agree with and admire Martin Luther without being a card-carrying Lutheran.

In *Why Christianity Must Change or Die,* John Shelby Spong poses the proposition, "Perhaps the time has come for Christians to begin asking What is God, rather than Who is God." Nice try, John. You're only one hundred and twenty-five years late. Mary Baker Eddy did that already. The first question in the chapter "Recapitulation"—a compendium of questions and answers that summarize her whole book—puts the question exactly that way. She answers it with nary a reference to gender.

> Question. — What is God? Answer. — God is incorporeal, divine, supreme, infinite Mind, Spirit, Soul, Principle, Life, Truth, Love.

Eddy closes *Science and Health* with a frontal assault on my old nemesis, "the Lord." She writes,

> In the following Psalm, one word shows though faintly, the light which Christian Science throws on the Scriptures by substituting for the corporeal sense, the incorporeal or spiritual sense of Deity:—

> Psalm XXIII

> [DIVINE LOVE] is my shepherd; I shall not want. [LOVE] maketh me to lie down in green pastures: [LOVE] leadeth me beside the still waters. [LOVE] restoreth my soul [spiritual sense]: [LOVE] leadeth me in the paths of righteousness for His name's sake. Yea, though I walk through the valley of the shadow of death, I will fear no evil: for [LOVE] is with me; [LOVE'S] rod and [LOVE'S] staff they comfort me. [LOVE] prepareth a table before me in the presence of mine enemies: [LOVE] anointeth my head with oil; my cup runneth over. Surely goodness and mercy shall follow me all the days of my life; and I will dwell in the house [the consciousness] of [LOVE] for ever.

Surprisingly, it wasn't until Larry and I moved south of the border that I tumbled to the fact that if substituting the word "Love" for "the Lord" works for the Twenty-Third Psalm, it can work in the First, the Second, on down to the Hundred and Fiftieth. Did I need detachment from the atmosphere of Midwestern Protestantism to feel free to take out a ballpoint pen and attack "sacred" pages?

I did so now with abandon, scrawling "LOVE" over every "the Lord" I found in my blue cloth-covered Bible. The theological freedom to take off my shoes and run barefoot in the sand now gave me Psalms that read, "O, Love, you've searched me and known me"; "O, Love, you've been our dwelling place in all generations"; "Blessed are they who walk in the law of Love ... they walk in Love's ways"; and "Because Love is at my right hand, I shall not be moved." Ahhhh! Those Psalms felt a lot better to me.

It was with this "barefoot state of mind," I now approached the statue of Our Lady of Guadalupe out on our little jetty. With my head cocked to one side and my eyes slightly squinted, a countenance that mirrored her own, I was open to a renewed acquaintance with her. I'd been eight years old when we'd first met, and that was a long, long time ago. Maybe it was time to reconsider a relationship with this lady.

I wasn't the only one whose presence she attracted out there on the beach. She had regular visitors, some in obviously organized groups, leaving bunches of fresh flowers, lighting a few candles. But more often it was a morning walker, paying her a visit out on the jetty, like touching the base, before turning back and making the return trek to a bungalow hotel on the other end of the beach.

Was this worship? I wrinkled my nose. While I'd long rejected worshipping a big Guy in the Sky, I wasn't ready to drop adoringly at the feet of a Big Woman, or Lady, or Mary. Who was Guadalupe, anyway? Was she just another version of the Virgin, who, like Santa Claus, has thousands of representations? Santa Claus represents an idea, not a person, right? Oh, perhaps there was a human being who gave rise to the concept of Santa Claus, but Santa himself has evolved into so much more. Could this be the case with Guadalupe? Could the concept into which the Virgin has evolved represent something much more than the young girl from Nazareth?

"If Guadalupe is Mary, why do they call her Guadalupe?" my friend wondered. "Why don't they just call her Mary, if that's her name?"

Good question, but the question you have to ask in return is who is they? If Guadalupe just speaks to Catholics or Christians, then it would stand to reason she should be called Mary. But she doesn't. If Juan Diego called her Tecuauhtlcupeuh, it was to appeal to the indigenous population, by whom she was adopted. Guadalupe as Guadalupe becomes so much more than just the Christian Mary. In *Science and Health,* Eddy uses the term "spiritual ideal," when referring to the image of the woman in Revelation—an image that sounds a lot like Guadalupe looks.

As an icon, the Virgin on the jetty didn't seem to make any stringent demands on those who came into her presence. Her back to the mainland, with tilted head and eyes cast downward,

105

she faced the waves and waited. Guadalupe—keeping silent watch. Covered with salt spray and plastic roses, she was just there. Waiting. Present. Available. Somehow, though, she commanded respect. Re-spect. A word that invites us to literally, "look again."

Was this what I had been seeking, hidden in plain sight? Was this the "feminine ideal" I'd ranted that was missing in action through a time line that stretched across eras? Maybe the question I should be asking about Guadalupe was like the question John Shelby Spong advocated asking about God. Perhaps my question should not be "Who are you, Lady?" but "What are you?" A spiritual ideal? The spiritual ideal? But then one has to ask, "An ideal what?"

SO, WHAT'S PERFECT?

"I hate these colors," says my friend Linda. "They don't go together at all!"

We're standing outside the *Oficina de Correos* near the town square in La Peñita.

"I don't know," I say. "You've got to love a country where post offices are painted raspberry pink and lime green."

At the market held each Thursday in this square, every color goes together, and nothing is quite perfect. It's an Indian market, a *tianguis,* and the fruit that farmers sell from the beds of their battered pickup trucks are often odd-sized and misshapen. Clumps of soil cling to golden globes of *mandarinas* and viridian-striped melons. Shreds of dried vegetation dangle off long yellow banana fingers. In this environment, where you want to clean all produce thoroughly, everyone has a bottle of Clorox on the kitchen sink.

It's the imperfections that prove something is truly authentic—the slubs left in the rugs and smaller *tapetes* woven by visiting Zapotecs from Oaxaca, their wares brilliant with the natural dyes of indigo, cochineal, and marigold. It's the slightly off-center design, the less-than-parallel lines, that distinguish hand-painted ceramics from mass-manufactured goods. Legions of garish coconut shell masks stare face up from the plaza bricks, not one like another, each a distinct little tiger or mermaid or iguana face, looking skyward—or up the skirt of the sober Cora Indian woman who offers them for sale.

But it is the Huichol, who emerge from villages hidden high in the Sierra, whose handwork is most dazzling, most individualized, and less likely to be pigeon-holed as "ideal." Elaborate and convoluted yarn paintings of brilliantly dyed threads or minutely detailed beadwork depict visions of the artist, his or her vision often inspired by ministrations of the sacred peyote. Scrawled across the back in black marker and less-than-perfect Spanish is the explanation of the symbols presented in the work. I buy small pieces and carry them home in one of the flat square purses woven by Huichol women. The purse itself consists of such a variety of hues and intricacy of design that I hang it on the wall when I get home. It's art, as much as the bead or yarn pictures.

My bookshelves, the tile floor beneath and the *equipale* table and chairs that furnish the cupola room are soon filled with what I find in the *tianguis*. I don't know if the colors go together. I just know they belong in the heart of my house.

CHAPTER 9

THE WARP AND WOOF
OF LIFE

You have to want to learn weaving.
You have to think that the work
you are doing was done by Takutsi Nakawe.
You have to ask for these thoughts
Yolanda, a Huichol weaver, quoted in *To Think with a Good Heart*

"Takutsi Nakawe" is the Huichol name for Grandmother Goddess of Growth and Creation. It was she who made the world out of twilight, appointed five other goddesses to preside over the four cardinal points and the center, and still maintains order in her creation. Takutsi Nakawe sees the big picture.

When a Huichol woman begins to weave, she takes the handloom she carries on her back and ties it to a tree branch. With one end in the tree and one end anchored in her lap, she sets long, strong, warp threads. With these as the basis, she begins weaving row upon row. The pattern of her piece may emerge gradually, but she recognizes it as complete before she ever begins the work. Stacy Schaefer's *To Think with a Good Heart* explores the world of *wixarika* women and their weaving. She paraphrases the weaver, Gabriela: "[The loom] is life. When I want to weave and I tie the loom up above [to a tree], my life is also tied up to the sky."

The warp threads of my life were set through the example of my grandmother. If any woman ever had her loom tied to the sky, Mama Hope did. Mother to eleven children and paragon to numerous grandchildren and great grandchildren, she was the center of a family that stretched across most of Oklahoma, Texas, Kansas, and Colorado. "What would Mama Hope say if she ever saw you acting like that?" The question never failed to stop me in my tracks, arrest the tantrum, stifle the sass. Mama Hope was good, solid-to-the-core good. It was the kind of good that rarely has to voice a rebuke or even raise an eyebrow. Mama Hope could just look a benign question: "Why would you possibly want to do that?" And suddenly, you didn't want to do whatever it was you were thinking of doing. You just wanted Grandma to be proud of you.

Grandmothers are special in Mexico, a country that has few if any pejorative terms for older women. While the word *madre* is rife with a myriad of meanings, good and bad, *abuela,* or the diminutive *abuelita,* is a term of tenderness. It's the label on the packages of chocolate for hot cocoa, a word usually said with a smile and a tilt of the head to one side. *Abuelita.* Little grandmother.

Mama Hope was diminutive. At just over five feet tall, her eleven children towered over her, girls as well as boys. It was Papa Hope who was large, over six feet tall. He was postmaster of the small Oklahoma town where the family finally settled, as well as local director of the Works Progress Administration during the Depression. That meant he had a job when many others did not, and that others depended on him to obtain the jobs they needed. From the stories I have heard and overheard from aunts and uncles, he was accustomed to having his way, on the schedule he himself chose. My mother's younger brother, the very youngest of the brood, recalls Papa Hope growing impatient while waiting for a break in traffic at an intersection. It seemed that one car after another kept coming, not going fast, but spaced just far enough apart to prevent his turning safely onto the road. Growing weary of the wait, he said, "My turn," pressed the accelerator, and entered the crossroads. Evidently there were no serious injuries in the resulting collision.

Papa Hope died before I knew him, shortly after my mother and father were married. My paternal grandfather passed on when I was four years old, and as neither of my grandmothers remarried, I grew up without a grandfather. I was extremely curious about these stern men who gazed out of family photo albums. So my ears pricked up when I heard aunts or uncles tell stories at family reunions. There was one overheard conversation I puzzled over for some time, but something told me not to ask for an explanation, at least from my mother. It happened this way.

Mama Hope subscribed to *Reader's Digest* and kept every one. They were ranged in a built-in bookcase behind her sofa, and when I'd visit in the summer, I would spend hours lying on the floor, working my way through copy after copy, finding a few things I was interested in, but mostly reading the jokes in the sections titled "Laughter the Best Medicine," and "Life in These United States." This went on even until I was in junior high. There just wasn't that much to do at Mama Hope's if my cousins weren't around. They were mostly boys, a couple my age, but most a few years older. The only girl relative close to my age, my cousin Jana, had a whole different way of looking at the boys than I did. This had become clear the Thanksgiving before.

"We've got to get ready to see our cousins," she'd said, rushing into the bedroom we shared a few hours prior to our all leaving for the annual Thanksgiving dinner at my Uncle Jimmy's house. Our holiday dinner was always a day late, on Friday, to give the more than ninety people who usually showed up a day's travel time to get to Oklahoma City. Jana moved towards the mirror, bumped me out of the way with her hip, and picked up a can of Aquanet. Disappearing momentarily into a cloud of sticky mist, she emerged to apply a coat of pale white lipstick.

"They're our cousins, Jana Sue," I protested. "It doesn't matter what we look like!"

She cast a glance of disdain my way, the kind a ninth-grade girl headed for high school shows for a just-finished seventh grader recently turned thirteen. She decided to be charitable with me, and explain. "Yes," she said archly, shaping the ends of her bouffant flip with practiced fingers and squinting at her image in the mirror. "They're cousins. But they're good for practice."

I was often mute in the face of such worldly sophistication. Jana had, after all, been a junior homecoming princess and had gone on actual car dates, while I was still arguing with Mom that yes, I did need a bra, if I were going to have to take off my clothes for gym class. She'd let me have one; I just needed to remember to wear it on gym days.

112

There was, however, one enviable advantage I held over Jana. My mother, converted as she was by my sure-to-go-to-hell Christian Science father, would let me dance. Jana's family was strict Southern Baptist. No dancing allowed—at least not with boys. But on the sly and in my company, Jana would practice jitterbug steps with any slightly animate object. It could be a door knob, a rocking chair, or the ideal partner she'd found one summer—a long piece of galvanized wire that was unraveling from the cyclone fence around the schoolyard across the street. She actually wanted my advice, because my mom and dad were members of several dance clubs and taught us steps when we were together in the kitchen. I didn't have that much opportunity to use those steps in real live social situations, but when I was with Jana, I flaunted the little knowledge I possessed as if it were occult power.

But Jana wasn't around this particular summer, and lacking any cousin-type company at all, I'd found refuge and entertainment on the carpet behind Mama Hope's sofa. The carpet was cool and unworn back there, and I was out of the way. Aunt Addie and Aunt Betty had no idea I was there when they sat down and began talking about my cousin Carla, who had just gotten a divorce. (Notice the nomenclature beginning with ABC? Do you think I'm actually going to use real names? Now Jana Sue—that is her real name, and she won't deny a word I've said about her.)

I didn't know Carla well. She was considerably older than I was, youngest daughter of one of Mom's much older sisters. Carla had come under a lot of criticism by family members of late, because this was the very first divorce in the whole family. No one could understand why she'd left the guy. He'd

113

treated her like a queen! He had wanted to be with her every minute, bought her gifts all the time, denied her nothing, and was always hugging her and calling her "Sweetie." She didn't even have to cook, because they went out for every meal. But still she just seemed lazy. Her house was a mess. She'd started neglecting her appearance and putting on weight. And then she'd left him! It made no sense.

"I know why she left him," Aunt Addie harrumphed. "He was just like Papa. First thing in the morning, noontime, three and four times a night. Every chance he could get at her. Mama was worn out, just plum wore out. I don't blame Carla at all. Who wants to live like that?"

It took me several years to figure that out. But the import of what Mama Hope went through became clearer and clearer the more I learned. Her first eight children were spaced two years apart. She was constantly nursing, probably as a form of birth control. Her only time alone was on Sunday mornings when Papa Hope would troop off to church with his brood of youngsters and Mama Hope remained behind to cook the Sunday dinner.

What must she have felt when, with five children at home, Papa Hope fell in love with another woman and was determined to run away with her?

It was her goodness that saved her family. The other woman refused to leave with Papa Hope. She couldn't do that, she said, to a woman as good as Melvina Hope. And with that decision, she herself cast her handloom skyward. Two women anchored in a good that was far above the mortal man who thought to control them both.

Mama Hope went on to have six other children. Though she loved each one fiercely, she had few other options than to remain in her home with Papa Hope. Her own father had suffered from rheumatoid arthritis, and as one of the oldest children, she left school after the fourth grade to stay home and help care for him while her mother supported the family as best she could. No wonder Mama Hope was determined that all her children, daughters as well as sons, attend college, learn to earn their own living, and be free to be who they really were. Like Takutsi Nakawe, she could see the big picture. She would agree with the Huichol woman Gabriela, who supports her family with her weaving: "You have to remain careful, thinking all of your life. You have to think with a good heart."

MOTHER'S EVENING PRAYER

Mary Baker Eddy

O gentle presence, peace and joy and power;
O Life divine, that owns each waiting hour,
Thou Love that guards the nestling's faltering flight!
Keep Thou my child on upward wing tonight.

Love is our refuge; only with mine eye
Can I behold the snare, the pit, the fall:
His habitation high is here, and nigh,
His arm encircles me, and mine, and all.

O make me glad for every scalding tear,
For hope deferred, ingratitude, disdain!
Wait, and love more for every hate, and fear
No ill,—since God is good, and loss is gain.

Beneath the shadow of His mighty wing;
In that sweet secret of the narrow way,
Seeking and finding, with the angels sing:
"Lo, I am with you alway,"—watch and pray.

No snare, no fowler, pestilence or pain;
No night drops down upon the troubled breast,
When heaven's aftersmile earth's tear-drops gain,
And mother finds her home and heav'nly rest.

CHAPTER 10

BEING THERE

Eighty percent of success is just showing up.
Woody Allen

"You don't have to say a word. You're here. That's all that matters." The young man who spoke to me was dressed in the boxy orange jumpsuit issued to inmates in California's Orange County jails. He spoke Spanish. So did I, sort of. That was, after all, the only reason I was there. "I don't speak his language and you do," my good friend Dessa had said to me again and again. She was a volunteer chaplain, determined to recruit my help. I wasn't interested. Truth be told in the spring of 1988, I couldn't have cared less about the people locked up in the three imposing buildings that abutted the Civic Center in downtown Santa Ana. Years before, I had lost one of my favorite aunts when she came across a mid-day intruder in her suburban home. She was murdered, leaving three young children. I had mentally set my jaw against "coddling" anyone who broke the law. If they were locked up, there was probably a good reason. That's where they belonged. That or ship them back to Mexico. End of story.

Not so for Dessa. "This guy has so many questions. He needs someone who can understand him, who can talk to him and give him some answers." She wheedled, nagged, hectored. For the sake of our friendship, I finally said "yes." Reluctantly.

I had no official standing like Dessa did, no white clip-on badge that would whisk me past administrative desks and directly into the bowels of the institution. I had to go in with regular visitors on a Saturday afternoon and wait with the common masses in the lobby of the IRC, the Intake Release Center. This was the facility with the highest security level, the first place an inmate came when he was booked, and the last place they found themselves prior to release or transfer to a real prison. It's a busy place with a huge visitors' lobby.

I looked around after I'd filled in the necessary paperwork and settled in to wait. If I hadn't been so caught up in the fact that it looked like I would be spending a whole Saturday on this errand for a friend, and boy, did she owe me big time, I might have caught a premonition of the great amount of time I would be spending in this lobby. Four years later, when I turned in my own chaplain's badge, I would have had contact with over 1,500 inmates behind these walls, a large majority of whom would have come from Mexico. I'd be leaving to embark on another volunteer career mentoring chaplains statewide and advocating prison reform. A few years later, I'd be traveling through the Americas, often as a guest speaker in correctional institutions. Over a period of ten years I visited at least forty-five of them. So that's where saying "yes" can lead.

But for that moment, at that time, I was more interested in getting through the appointment I had made without being sick to my stomach. I'd never been good meeting strangers, and meeting a stranger who was behind bars was especially intimidating. Neither was I particularly comfortable in the brightly lit lobby, teeming with what I then imagined to be the dregs of humanity. If these people weren't criminals themselves, they were the closest thing to it. They were the friends and families of criminals. There were a lot of them.

It was the Spanish-speakers who brought the largest entourages. Wives and grandmothers, girlfriends, uncles and aunts, babies in arms, children crawling over and under the banks of molded plastic seats bolted to the floor, young girls smoothing the creases of their first communion dresses. I didn't know then what I do now about jails in Mexico. Anything a prisoner needs—that includes clothing, food, and personal items—must be provided from outside. You go to jail in Mexico, you had better have a family on the outside who will feed you—or you'd better make friends with someone inside who does.

Flash forward to my second summer living here. It was Jackie's girlfriends in La Peñita and Guayabitos who carried her food fit for a diabetic, blankets, sheets, a down vest, books, and even a toilet seat north to the jail in Compostela. That was when Jackie's ex-husband issued a *demanda* on her, and she was summarily locked up. Domestic troubles can turn nasty with sudden swiftness, and the first to make a criminal accusation gets to see the other hauled to the "hoosegow," that Old West term for the county jail. It's a corruption of the Spanish *juzgado,* which means "judged." Corruption, all right—guilty until proven innocent is the rule of law in Mexico, thank you Emperor Napoleon and the Code you instituted for most of the world. For five weeks our friend was confined to a Pine-Sol scented, bare necessities jail yard with six other inmates less than half her age, who, to their credit, promptly and tenderly adopted her as *abuelita,* little grandmother.

Mexican jails in many cases are not as frightening as spaghetti westerns would have us believe. Not that I'm recommending a stay in one, but the Centro de Rehabilitación Social Feminil (CRSF) outside of Guadalajara was not at all intimidating once you got inside. Maybe it was the children's swing set on the green lawn just past the entry gate that gave off a different vibe than what I'd been used to seeing in women's prisons in the U.S. Or maybe it was the rose garden, or the fresh juice bar at one end of the covered central patio.

There was no comparison between this and the women's institution at Marysville, Ohio, the first women's prison I visited as a Christian Science lecturer. It was a formidable relic of the nineteenth century, complete with crenellated towers. There's a similar prison I'd later visit outside Elmira, New York, a relic of the Civil War.

But those institutions with all their antiquated fixtures and smoke-stained bricks can at least be termed picturesque, in a gruesome sort of way. They offer more opportunity for human contact than the sterile new facilities that are models of sensory deprivation in the extreme. Not only are the newer buildings barren on the inside, but usually they're built in far out-of-the-way locations, in desert or mountain landscape that present a real hardship for families without a car that is trustworthy enough to make the trip. Hourly wage earners with limited finances have to take days off work for the privilege of an hour or so visit. I've stood waiting in a parking lot outside of Soledad Prison in California's Central Valley with women who had scrimped and saved for months to take off time to travel to see a son, a boyfriend, a father or husband. Their presence was important to the men inside. When inmates believe no one cares any more, they have little to lose. Violence increases and crazy things happen. The Virgin-spirit needs to be there.

The warden at the Guadalajara Women's Prison, the CRSF, was definitely a one-in-herself type of woman. "Fierce mother" are the words that come to mind when I think of her. Her charges were mostly women left behind by the men of Michoacan who had traveled north to the States. They were incarcerated for resorting to the oldest profession to support the families that had been abandoned. Or they were there for being burros, transporting narcotics in a way that would defile body and soul. One of my prized possessions is a slender volume given to me by the warden, the autobiography of one of the current inmates, published in book form by the University of Guadalajara. There were many such volumes, many such stories, all ending with their time at CRSF. The series of books was a result of a literacy and therapy project run by the University. Never have I seen a similar project on such a scale in the United States.

But I either digress or jump ahead. I visited the prison in Guadalajara in 2001, and the Compostela jail in 2008, as one with long experience of prisons on my resume. But in 1988, north of the border, in my first visit to any jail, ever, I sat waiting in the lobby, judgment in my heart, my heart in my throat, and my throat dry with fear. I watched the clock with hundreds of other would-be visitors. They didn't bring tamales or *posole*. They brought love and support. And patience—lots and lots of patience.

We waited. Then waited hours more. There were only so many provisions for visitors, and small numbers were admitted for short periods of time. The Spanish language swirled around me, and I began feeling a panicky sense of inadequacy.

What was I doing there? I didn't speak this kind of Spanish. It had been years since I'd spoken Spanish at all, other than to recognize items on a menu or give occasional direction to a gardener. How was I supposed to communicate with someone about prayer, the Bible, God's plan and purpose? I realized I didn't even know how the Lord's Prayer went in Spanish.

But it was too late. The name of my inmate was called. I rose and walked across to the heavy steel door I'd seen so many others pass through. It slammed shut behind me and the one I was facing opened. I followed the other visitors up the metal stairs, where we took assigned seats on round metal stools banked before formidably thick windows that separated us from the inmates we were to see. The glass before me looked as if someone had been finger-painting in spittle. The air was close, smelling of child sweat, cheap toiletries, and tennis shoes. There were candy wrappers lodged in the corners of the shallow stainless steel counter before me. I didn't want to think what might be stuck to the underside.

I set out the Spanish copy of *Science and Health* and a copy of *la Santa Biblia* in front of me. It was my way of identifying myself with my friend Dessa, and I saw the eyes of the young man sitting on the other side of the glass light up in recognition of the books. He smiled at me and indicated the phone set I was to use hanging on the wall to one side of the booth. He already had his in hand. Mine was dirty, but I brought it to my ear, promising myself an immediate trip to the ladies room at a nearby Nordstrom's as soon as I got out of there.

"*Hola,*" I heard the tinny echo of his voice through the ear piece.

"*Hola,*" I replied, and smiled uncertainly.

Then there was a torrent of Spanish. It rat-a-tat-tatted through the handset I held to my ear and might as well have passed right out the other side of my head. I didn't understand a thing. He paused and waited for a response. What had happened? My mouth didn't work! I realized with horror that every word—and I do mean every word—of Spanish I ever knew had left my head. The cord on the handset was short. I couldn't even cradle it under my chin and talk with my hands. I stared at him wide-eyed, scared and speechless. I shrugged, gave him what I hoped was a smile, and opened my right hand to him, palm facing upward.

He took a deep breath, smiled and spoke in slow clear Spanish: "You don't have to say a word. You're here. That's all that matters." In measured tones with many pauses to make sure I was getting what he said—and by now I was able to listen intelligently if not answer effectively—he poured out a heartfelt flood of gratitude—thanks to God, thanks to Jesus, thanks to Dessa, thanks to the author of *Science and Heath,* thanks to the people who had made Dessa's visits possible. He didn't have questions, he didn't want a long discussion. What he wanted was someone who understood him to accept his gratitude. He needed to tell his story. I was the one who showed up to listen. Nothing was really required of me except to be present. Available. Like Guadalupe.

The amazing grace-filled one-certain-thing about the feminine spiritual ideal whatever form it takes and wherever and however it happens to appear is that nothing is required of the ideal but to be there. It doesn't lift swords, slay dragons, throw down thunderbolts. The feminine ideal—call it Virgin, call it Mother, Gentle Presence, Grace, Love—just shows up. It's there, and things change.

Maybe what changes is our perspective. A few years later, sitting on my usual metal seat in the IRC, I looked with horror at George, an inmate I'd been seeing for several months. He was covered in lacerations. His first words were to reassure me. I was not to worry.

"It was only to teach me a lesson," he said. He'd been caught alone in the shower by a rival gang. "They could have killed me, but they didn't."

There was nothing for me to say, except, "Thank God."

We just sat together, heads bowed, reaching out to a Love that both of us intuitively knew was more powerful than hate-filled humans. Our times together over the next months were often spent that way. He went through his trial. It was a capital offense, but he was spared the death penalty. The last time I saw him was just before he was to be transferred to a state prison for a life sentence. He was cheerful. He felt a tangible change of something had taken place. "You know those guys who cut me?" he asked. "Guess what. One of them bought me a candy bar last night. He wished me luck at State. I never would have thought it."

A raft of caring emails doesn't do anything for an invalid, except letting him know he's loved. Sitting beside someone and letting them cry, being there when they come out of anesthesia, showing up unexpectedly at a neighbor's with a plate of sweet rolls, making actual eye contact with the begging woman in the street even if your own pocket is empty, listening to an inmate's story—everyone has the chance to be a surrogate Virgin—to be there. Sometimes we're willing. Sometimes we're not. But where there's the faintest whiff of compassion, She's there. And that says it all.

LA MICHOACANA
—She's everywhere! She's everywhere!

I am addicted to frozen limeade on a stick. Just writing about one now makes me want to head for La Avenida, which is the four-block main street in La Peñita. There is at least one ice cream store on every one of those four blocks, most presided over by one of the most ubiquitous feminine icons in Mexico. The little plump Indian maid above the entrance is "La Michoacana."

What we call "supper" in Texas is a moveable feast in La Peñita. The main Mexican meal is la comida, a substantial multi-course meal eaten between two and four in the afternoon. *La cena* comes in the evening, when people tend to graze from one street stand to another consuming *tacos, tortas, hamburguesas, hotdogs, papas fritas, sopes*. But at the end of the evening, it's the ice cream stores that are crowded. *Paletas* at La Michoacana are so much more than mere popsicles, those non-descript sugar-water concoctions that require lurid dyes to tell you what flavor you're supposed to be tasting. La Michoacana paletas are fresh fruit frozen in their own juices, solidified into little icy slices of heaven, a streetside sorbet, with flavor as eye-popping as the colors they come in. Bend over the freezer bin in one of these local purveyors and you're met with a kaleidoscope of choice, all depending on the season and what is absolutely fresh.

La Michoacana is an unregistered trademark, open for anyone to use, so the stores are as individual as the owners. It makes for a unique experience every time, but I've never been disappointed. I plan on sampling each and every flavor at each and every ice cream store—someday. But first, just one more *agua de limón, por favor*. Ah! As it says on the sign: es *natural!*

CHAPTER 11

THE SEED
WITHIN ITSELF

And it came to pass, that, when Elisabeth heard the salutation of Mary,
the babe leaped in her womb; and Elisabeth was filled with the Holy Ghost:
And she spake out with a loud voice, and said,
Blessed art thou among women, and blessed is the fruit of thy womb.
Luke 1:41,42

In a hidden cave sanctuary at the top of a hill near the present day Basilica of the Virgin of Guadalupe, there is a series of symbols carved into the rock. The representation is unmistakable. This is earth as vulva, open and ready for the falling semen of rain. To watch the overnight growth of anything that is planted during the rainy season is to know that the land which is Mexico is a fertile womb indeed, a womb that is always full and is always bringing forth. Cobblestone streets turn green and furry, coco palms spring up through the grates above drainage ditches. Overnight, pale fresh leaves appear on shrubbery and trees. Mexico is a place where any seed grows.

One of the more frequent questions I get from friends up north about moving down here is, "What do you do all day?" The concept that there is daily work to be done and all the normal paraphernalia of existence to contend with south of the border as well as north seems as foreign to some as Mexico itself. Back in my other life there were some days that all I did was answer the phone. Here, I answer the door.

It was especially hectic when we first arrived, before we learned not to spread the schedules of service and cleaning people throughout the week, but to dedicate just a few days to frenzied activity. I look at the journal I kept during that time and find Chano arriving six mornings a week for three weeks straight at 7:00 a.m. sharp to paint our ironwork purple and put a lot of plants in pots. During that time we also had the tile man who put up the mural in the cupola and fixed the kitchen counter. Then there were the people who delivered bottled water, the teenager who serviced the swimming pool, the garbage men—all of whom made twice a week appearances at different times of the day.

Hilda fought a thrice-weekly battle with masonry dust on floors, wielding her string mop and a big bucket of Fabuloso, the Mexican cleaning solution that comes in a myriad of Kool-Aid colors and fragrances. Ringing the bell at the front gate or calling from the street, there was Priscilla who sold pickles, the guy with the truck full of watermelons, some other guys selling silver chains and watches door to door, Maria bringing me pineapples from her farm, three lawyers serving papers on the people who lived here before, a grizzled old guy in a pickup selling fresh relics *("Auténticos, Señora. Te lo juro"),* people asking about the lot for sale next door, the exterminator (did you know that concrete gets termites?!), the workers who reburied our fresh water pipe more than two inches below the driveway—

all of this besides much welcomed visits from neighbors and friends.

But when people ask, "What do you do?" I hear, "What are you producing? What are you bringing forth? Is there actually something that the world will remember you for that will serve to justify your existence on the planet?" To be honest, that may merely be the self-accusatory little voice in my head that crops up from time to time ever since I decided no, I wasn't going to have children. Maybe writing this book is a defensive act. At last I can respond with something definite to those people who ask me how I fill my days, now that we've "settled in" down here.

Every move to a new place requires learning the ropes, getting to know things. Knowledge of a place implies intimacy with it—the ins and outs, Where to go for This, What to do when That happens. You become a part of a place, and it becomes a part of you. For Larry, lacking language skills, the move was traumatic at first. He'd always joked that if he'd been born a hundred years before, in New England, he'd still be sitting in Philadelphia watching the History Channel. For him, "virgin territory" is the set of channels above 400. A pioneer he's not. That's why I was convinced that this move, this spontaneous major adjustment to our lives carried out in perfect concert and agreement between the two of us, had to be, if not divinely ordained, at least inspired along those lines.

We sold our California house, maybe not at the top of the real estate market, but slightly on the downhill side after the crest. Like most Americans, it was our major investment, aside from some funds in retirement accounts. What set us apart was that we owned it outright. Haven't I said that we were obedient children? While our two sets of parents held diametrically opposite political views, there was one thing they all agreed on. Pick a house you love and work like crazy to pay off the loan. You can owe on other real estate, but you must own your own home. Neither Larry nor I are known for our financial acumen, but that parental counsel, plus having no children, staying married to each other, and bringing in a steady paycheck can look like genius in retrospect. It certainly counterbalanced some other decisions we made. With what we netted from the sale of the house in California, we bought the house in Mexico, paid off every debt we had, and bought a car that would last at least ten years.

"It's not a full-sized Hummer," I kept saying defensively to our friends. "It's more a *Hummercita*, the little one. It's not that big urban assault monster." We'd done the research, and the Hummer 3 was really the best vehicle for us at the best price. But time after time, I felt obliged to explain our action. The defense became easier as we got better acquainted with our new environment: the square top provided extra shade from intense tropical sun; the tight turning radius maneuvered the rugged little cul-de-sac at the end of our street with nary a stop-and-back-up; the four-wheel drive package handled the precipitous jungle roads that laced up through the hills and down to the beaches as if they were flatland farm roads; the high clearance let us straddle rut-defined back roads with barely a tummy tickle. Besides all this, the gas mileage wasn't horrible and it fit in that underground basement/garage, which, while it was vast and roomy, had a very low-profile entryway. Surprisingly, Hummercita is shorter than most large SUVs. But of course, most important of all, there was a General Motors dealership and service center in Puerto Vallarta. With a GM product, we knew we were safe. We could depend on a rock-solid company that would be around forever.

Can we pick 'em or what? There were other "brilliant" choices we made.

Years before, we had invested our IRA funds in what looked like another sure-fire proposition, a brand new community bank in a booming area of Southern California. It was scheduled to open the morning of September 12, 2001. Despite that inauspicious date, it had eventually prospered. "Sometime," we told ourselves, "like in 2008 or so, when we really retire, a big bank like Wells Fargo or Bank of America is going to come along and give us a lot of money for our stock in that little bank." We are no longer holding our breath in anticipation. Maybe by 2018 that stock will recover.

Another stellar investment decision we made was revealed as a Ponzi scheme about seven months before the September 2008 financial meltdown, when other such schemes came to light. Like the true trailblazers we've always been, we watched our nest egg go "Dubai-bye." We were left with a stunningly decimated balance in our assets column.

What do I know for certain? It was a question I'd begun asking myself over and over again, not just about our new surroundings, but about life in general. It seemed that everything I'd deemed dependable hadn't been.

The noble country I loved had become identified with some very ignoble acts and attitudes. Family camaraderie and conversation revolved either around a business I was no longer a part of or around offspring that I didn't have. Church might have brought us together, but even that topic was off-limits, as each of us held different opinions about the direction the Christian Science Mother Church was taking. Besides, for some of my family, it looked as though I'd renounced the church and maybe even had converted to Catholicism. What was all that virgin business, anyway? Our investments had crumbled, leaving us with little cash on hand. Underlying it all, my health seemed to have slipped into a definite "iffy" category. When it was good, it was only pretty good, and when it was bad, it was horrid. It looked like I couldn't be sure of anything anymore.

But despite all this, far from feeling displaced, fearful, and homesick, I was gradually settling into a sense of wellbeing. It sounds crazy, but it's true. Perhaps it had something to do with that view off the verandah, the sense of being folded against the bosom of the Sierra Vallejo. Maybe it was the *estero* behind the house, rising and falling with the tide, "still waters" that provided a shimmering reflection of birds and sky and trees. Possibly it was the moon and stars that now swept down with an immediate intimacy I hadn't felt since girlhood, when my sister Emily and I would sit out on a quilt in the backyard, counting meteors and pointing out constellations. After twenty years in urban Southern California, I'd forgotten how close and how vast the night sky could be. Everything below seemed dwarfed in comparison.

While the wonders of Mother Nature were comforting, there was also a different mental atmosphere I found in Mexico. Mexicans are long on social capital if not in concrete assets. Extended adopted families and friendship networks multiplied for us as we settled into the rhythm of small town society. Greetings and departures involved thoughtful rituals of acknowledgment. Every person present received either kisses or handshakes, coming and going. Children were indulged, but unfailingly polite to elders in social situations. Smiles to strangers were always returned, and even among the poorest, a quiet dignity prevailed with most exchanges. Even the act of buying a shrimp taco on the street was suffused with an attention to detail that honored both buyer and seller—as well as the shrimp itself.

As everything I had counted on before fell away; that which really mattered seemed to grow clearer. I was more and more convinced that what I was searching for, the certainty I could know, wasn't out there, but already a part of me. "Self-complete" would be the term I'd choose to best describe the feeling growing inside me, fruit of the seeds of self-knowledge. Wasn't that the gist of every spiritual journey metaphor, from *The Alchemist* to Oz? "There's no place like home. There's no place like home," the story goes, and you click your ruby slippers together and find that happiness lies in your own backyard. My backyard was in Mexico now, and for me in my new environment, the Virgin of Guadalupe seemed a visual expression of self-completeness and self-knowledge. In her downcast expression and sideways glance, she seemed to say to me, "Don't worry. You'll get it. It's right here before you."

"What if we hadn't sold the house?" I queried Larry. Neither the moon nor the stars, let alone the Virgin, were working their magic on him. He was in a stoic sort of mourning. "If we hadn't moved when we did," I continued, "we'd still be in California, not able to sell our house even for less than we bought it. We'd still be liable for property taxes, insurance, registering cars for exorbitant fees, paying state personal income tax, and paying more for gasoline than anywhere else in the country. The only thing cheaper in California than the rest of the U.S. is Two-Buck Chuck at Trader Joe's."

I was referring to the passable and palatable Charles Shaw label of red and white wines at my most favorite grocery store in the whole world. If there's anything I miss about California, it's shopping at Trader Joe's. I'd had occasion to visit one in Santa Fe recently, and found that there, out of the State of California, Charles Shaw sold for $2.99 a bottle instead of $1.99. You'd have to drink a lot of wine to justify the other expenses of living in California to make up that difference. It wouldn't happen in my life time.

Larry rolled his eyes, agreed, and reached for the remote. Okay. So be it. I had to leave Larry to work through his own issues of self-worth and life purpose. I knew from experience he'd eventually find an answer, usually in the shape of something that involved an engine, wheels, and a gearbox. The "V" for his victory doesn't stand for Virgin. It stands for "Vroom."

As for me, I silently savored and pondered a growing sense of sweetness inside me. I had known bitter. Its sharp acid taste had been on my tongue and in my belly during the time leading up to our move and the crisis-ridden time of transition afterward. Why weren't these new crises affecting me in a similar fashion? Why wasn't I torn up inside with thoughts of resentment and plots of revenge? No. Instead I was happy, with a joy that needed expression. So I painted, I danced, I tasted new things that people offered. Sometimes I felt as if the earth around me was swollen to bursting with the same happiness—as if life was a song ready to erupt in a cascade of melody.

So it seemed perfectly natural one day when the man who sold me fruits and vegetables broke into a joyful ode at the top of his voice, dedicated to the perfect tomato he held up for my inspection. I could identify with his urge. Enveloped in sunshine and bed linens hung out to dry, my own song bubbled up and outward one bright afternoon.

"Cucurrucucú, Palo-o-o-o-oma!"

I only knew one line of the plaintive song that pleads with the dove, but there was such a satisfactory guttural trill to the "r"s, and making the sound of long "u"s and "o"s, my lips naturally took the shape of a kiss. I was in love with the world. That was one thing I knew for sure and certain.

Was this what being pregnant was like? I'd never been "with child," but something was developing inside me. If Coatlicue could be impregnated by a ball of feathers when she was sweeping the temple, couldn't I sing to a dove while I hung out the laundry? I was so happy to be able to carry those sheets and pillowcases up from the basement, to have the strength to lift them to the line and clip them there with the funny little clothespins bought in the market. Wow! This was conceiving things in a whole different way. Housework had always seemed dead end and tedious, but even its repetition seemed to me a blessing. From somewhere I was getting a perspective on life as a cycle, where the beginning flows into the end, only to be reborn as the beginning once more. Every day, it seemed to me, was a brand new beginning, pregnant with possibilities, a new adventure ripe to burst on the scene fully formed.

BLESSED AMONG WOMEN

A Modern Translation of the Magnificata

And Mary said,
I'm bursting with God-news
I'm dancing the song of my Savior God.
God took one good look at me, and look what happened—
I'm the most fortunate woman on earth!
What God has done for me will never be forgotten,
The God whose very name is holy, set me apart from all others.
His mercy flows in wave after wave
On those who are in awe before him.
He bared his arm and showed his strength,
Scattered the bluffing braggarts.
He knocked tyrants off their high horses,
Pulled victims out of the mud.
The starving poor sat down to a banquet;
The callous rich were left out in the cold.
He embraced his chosen child, Israel;
He remembered and piled on the mercies, piled them high.
It's exactly what he promised,
Beginning with Abraham and right up to now.

Eugene Peterson, The Message, Luke 1: 46–55

CHAPTER 12

MARISABIA

To live alone—to have no obligation
that would hinder the freedom to study—
not even a communal murmur that would intrude
on the peaceful silence of my books.

Sor Juana Inés de la Cruz

It is December 2009, and my friend Jane and I are wandering the aisles of the massive Feria Internacional de Libros in Guadalajara, the second largest book fair in the world. It is an annual eight-day event where almost two thousand publishers from all over the world exhibit their wares in a hall that covers 40,000 square meters. That is about ten acres, and we're tired, overwhelmed not only by the size of the space, but by the crowd and the level of enthusiasm. Most of the people here are under thirty.

I retreat to the precincts of some university press exhibit and make a connection with a bright young woman, one who's been dead for over three hundred years. It is her name emblazoned across a pure white volume two inches thick that catches my eye: *Sor Juana Inés de la Cruz: Obras Completas. Her complete works in one book,* I think. *Wow!* I lift it up to take a closer look. Volume

I, it says. Beneath it lie Volume II, Volume III, and Volume IV. Wow, indeed! I had heard her work described as voluminous. The publisher's display brings the fact home. This woman was smart—and prolific. All of it was accomplished before her mid-forties. Not just "Wow!" Whew! I've just turned sixty and am trying to get just one book written.

Marisabia. Mary Sage. That's the Spanish term for a female know-it-all. I'm afraid I probably acted like one when I was very young. Until I was seven years old, we lived on a red-brick paved street in an old part of Lubbock, just a block off Broadway. There were no other children around to play with, and my social skills were formed through talking with our neighbors, all of whom were elderly. To their credit, they seemed to think I was brilliant, a purview I carried with me into the first grade and beyond. It had disappeared by the time I hit puberty, as is often the case with young women, though mine got a definite setback around the time I was ten. It had to do with an old man that everyone trusted. More about that later, but it is one thing I have in common with Sor Juana, who is, perhaps the quintessential *marisabia.*

Her picture graces the 200-peso note. That would put the image of Sor Juana Inés de la Cruz in greater circulation than that of Guadalupe. Maybe. At least Sor Juana's experience of having her picture engraved on national currency hasn't paralleled that of Susan B. Anthony, whose coin in the United States now serves as either an object of curiosity or an irritating inconvenience without a designated compartment in the cash drawer. For a seventeenth-century nun, Sor Juana really gets around.

Of course, she was not always a nun. Juana Inés de Asbaje y Ramirez was born in New Spain (the old name for Mexico) in November 1648. She learned to read when she was three years old, sneaking off to school with her older sister. At the age of eight, she wrote her first publicly performed literary work, and prior to becoming a teenager, she mastered Latin in only twenty lessons. When she was fourteen, she became a maid of honor to the wife of the Spanish Viceroy in Mexico City, and delighted the court with her erudition and learning. But at twenty-one she entered a convent because in order to continue her life of writing, musical composition, scientific and mathematical studies and vast correspondence with the other literary lights of the day, that was the only option available to her. That's when she became Sor Juana Inés de la Cruz, a daughter of the church and a bride of Christ.

She was not particularly religious. Many scholars (mostly males) have speculated on her reasons for going into a convent—did she have an unhappy love affair? But she wrote and said repeatedly that she only wanted to be by herself—happily studying, without having to fix dinner for anyone or share the bed of a demanding husband.

"Ah, then!" others exult. "She must have been a lesbian!" Her rapturous love poetry is indeed addressed not to any man, but to several women who acted as her patronesses. It is, however, doubtful that any enduring physical relationship could have been indulged with so many witnesses constantly surrounding her. For her "cell" in the convent was in actuality a salon, where she received daily visits from anyone in the upper classes of seventeenth century Mexico City interested in having an erudite conversation. Sor Juana had opinions and never failed to voice them, either verbally, or more often in her prodigious writings. How did she get away with that? Well, she didn't. Not for long. This is how it happened.

Picture this. You're Sor Juana and you're having an interesting conversation with friends who have called on you in your cell at the convent. These are men and women of Mexico City who share an intellectual bent, and the subject is a theological point. As usual, you state your perspective clearly, logically, and with an articulate skill that draws admiration from others. One of your friends makes a request: "Sor Juana, you've obviously given this matter a good deal of thought, and you express yourself so well on the subject. Might I have a draft of your ideas, so I can study them further?" He happens to be a bishop, one who has supported and defended you in the past, so you hate to refuse him.

"The paper is incomplete!" you respond. "I've just been jotting my thoughts down, and they are far from ready to be presented publicly."

"Oh, this is something just between the two of us. I would never dream of making them generally available. They are just for my own personal study. Oh, please, do let me have a copy. You can trust me completely." *(Heh, heh, heh.)*

Because you are, after all a nun, and a very good girl, you acquiesce, and send the Bishop of Puebla your incomplete work, warts and all.

The next thing you know, your rough little essay appears in print, just as it was written. Alongside it is a letter, which appears to be written by one of your sisters in the order of

140

Carmelites, a certain Sor Filotea, though she is unfamiliar to you. Sor Filotea proceeds to chastise you for stepping outside your role as nun and daring to express your opinion on matters that should not concern women at all. It is also obvious, she continues, from the rudimentary nature of your essay, the incomplete sentences and far-from polished language you use, that you don't have the capabilities to express yourself well at all. But isn't that common for all women? Give up trying to be a scholar, Sor Filotea counsels, and devote your life to what you are best suited—the quiet contemplation of Christ and ministry to others.

Perfidy! You have been twice deceived! Not only has your trusted friend done what he promised not to do, but hiding behind the persona of a woman, he has rebuked you as a woman for being what you are. Double betrayal! Sor Juana's response, *Respuesta a Sor Filotea,* is a classic text in defense of woman's intelligence and right to education. It is acknowledged as a literary work of genius, full of double meanings, ironic twists, and humor that is revealed level upon level depending on the familiarity the reader has with Bible texts and cultural mores of the 1600s. She addresses "Sor Filotea," sardonically and with exaggerated humility, but also takes a familiar tone that would have not been possible had she been writing directly to a bishop of the Church, as in fact she was. She takes the opportunity to gender-switch, imploring Sor Filotea to "imagine herself a man." But she also draws parallels to her own situation and that of the Virgin Mary, making word plays on, for instance, the heavenly "signs" that foretold Mary's experience and her, Sor Juana's, own present day "insignificant" life. In another place, she compares the magnificat that the Virgin was inspired to raise in praise with Sor Filotea's own "magnificently written" critique of Sor Juana's work.

Response to Sor Filotea has a distinct place in the library of feminist thought. It rises head and shoulders above the vast amount of her other work, which is compiled in the four large volumes I've found at the book fair. That Mexico now gives her such honor, that her image is still (ahem) "current," speaks volumes itself for the respect accorded women's learning. Though Mexico is often depicted as a *macho* society—and I'm not disputing that at all—there are as many Mexicans who can quote the first words of her poem "Hombres Necios," as there are Americans who can quote verses from the prologue of *Chaucer's Canterbury Tales*. Maybe it's because the first verse of "Hombres Necios" is printed right on the Mexican two hundred peso note, just under the words "Banco de Mexico."

However, *La Respuesta* was Sor Juana's last great effort. Shortly after its publication in 1695, she sold all her musical and scientific instruments, as well as the library of over 4,000 books she had collected. Giving the proceeds to charity, she renewed her religious vows, and devoted herself to serving the poor alongside the other sisters in her order.

Three months later she died while nursing the sick during a cholera epidemic.

Did the bishop's criticism indeed strike some vulnerable spot in the psyche of this incredibly intelligent woman? In her mid-forties with a large body of work under the girdle of her habit, it is unlikely that the bishop's words would have spawned a cloud of self-doubt in the heart of one so grounded. It is a question scholars have puzzled over for centuries. Her seeming capitulation has been a disappointment to feminists, and has provided fuel for those who would say, "See? Told you so!"

Perhaps there is a simpler explanation for Sor Juana's retreat and subsequent demise. Maybe it wasn't a retreat at all. I have another friend, a woman much older than I who has seen her share of battles on the women's intellectual freedom front. It's a war that can seem tediously repetitious. "Sometimes," she confided to me, "you wonder if things will ever change. You just get worn out dealing with dodos."

HOMBRES NECIOS
OR
YOU MEN!

Selected Verses
Sor Juana Inés de la Cruz
English translation by Electa Arenal and Amanda Powell

Hombres necios que acusáis　　　You foolish and unreasoning men
a la mujer sin razón　　　Who cast all blame on women,
sin ver que sois la ocasión　　　Not seeing you yourselves are
cause
de lo mismo que culpáis　　　Of the same faults you accuse:

Si con ansia sin igual　　　If, with eagerness unequaled,
solicitáis su desdén　　　You plead against women's disdain,
¿por qué queréis que obren bien　　　Why require them to do well
si las incitáis al mal?　　　When you inspire them to fall?

Combatís su resistencia　　　You combat their firm resistance,
y luego, con gravedad　　　And then solemnly pronounce
decís que fue liviandad　　　That what you've won through
diligence
lo que hizo la diligencia.　　　Is proof of women's flightiness.

CHAPTER 13

LITTLE TINY
FOOTPRINTS

When April with his showers sweet with fruit
The drought of March has pierced unto the root
And bathed each vein with liquor that has power
To generate therein and sire the flower; ...
Then do folk long to go on pilgrimage
Canterbury Tales, Chaucer

The Spanish word for "pilgrim" is *peregrino,* and a pilgrimage is a *peregrinación.* Birds make *peregrinaciones* when they fly north or south, and many of the faithful in La Peñita make a *peregrinación* to Talpa each spring. They do it to honor Nuestro Virgen Rosario de Talpa. Her festival goes on for ten days at the beginning of May, a time marked by the departure of most gringos and the commencement of four-in-the-morning firework celebrations, a felicitous coincidence, if ever there was one.

It is the tiny Virgin of Talpa, not of Guadalupe, who is front and center in the sanctuary of what may be the ugliest church in Mexico. She floats in the middle of a vast unadorned wall painted the color of the cotton gin machinery my dad manufactured—sea mist green—a shade that exactly matched the walls of the school-room cafeteria where I grew up. This may explain the negative feeling I get when entering the precincts of said sanctuary.

The church on the square in La Peñita has been under perpetual construction since who knows when. It does have a roof, a beautiful *boveda* ceiling, which bodes well for what the finished project may look like, but the huge hulking building that crouches to one side of the central plaza is marked more by the smell of wet concrete than by incense and candles. There always seems to be a huge pile of sand and empty buckets of Comex paint around the entry. The floor is a rough, paint-splotched cement slab, and noise from the far-from-permanent pews bounces off unfinished walls and stairways-to-nowhere when anyone sits down or shifts in his seat. As is the case with most communal buildings in the town, the services of any qualified architect were dispensed with, and the local contractors charged with completing the job have overcompensated in the amount of structural support and thickness of walls. When in doubt, add more concrete. Not only is this church ugly, it's also built to last.

The Virgin of Talpa, by comparison, is fragile. She's literally made of straw. The original shrine built in her honor lies some fifty miles inland from our coast, up in the mountains that rise behind Puerto Vallarta. You can reach it by car on a new road in a matter of hours. Pilgrims from La Peñita take an alternate route, a back road that is mainly dirt and intermittent cobblestone, that cuts behind the Sierra Vallejo and emerges from the jungle at San Juan de Abajo, an inland town rarely visited by Puerto Vallarta tourists. From there, pilgrims follow another back road up into the mountains until they reach the

146

crest of a hill, join the paved road, and are poised for a steep descent down *La Espina del Diablo* into Talpa itself. There are some who do it on their knees.

"Not me!" insists Paz, assistant to the dentist I'm consulting. "I drive the car that hands out water and food. But you won't catch me out on the road all that way! Not on a horse, not even walking. Some of these people, can you imagine, *Señora*, they strap *nopales* to their legs, so the spines will press into their flesh as they walk on their knees. Ay, they must be compensating for some very big sins." *Nopales* are the flat leaves of the prickly pear cactus. I shudder appreciatively, and Paz continues. "For me, in honor of the Virgin in Zapopan, in Guadalajara where I was born, I made it one time from the front door of the church to the altar on my knees. I still have scars! Never again. It is easier to be good."

When I visit Talpa, we drive—asphalt and air conditioning all the way. I bought a postcard across the street from the shrine. It's an image of the tiny Virgin with the triangle of a dress spread out beneath her. Unlike Guadalupe, there are no modest, downwardly cast eyes. This little woman looks defiantly straightforward. She looks like a virgin who is used to getting her way.

The story of her appearance is much like those of other Virgin sightings in rural Mexico. Where else would it start but in a farmer's field? This particular farmer thought he had found a child's toy, a diminutive straw figure, perhaps a foot tall. He carried it home, and a few days later presented it to the daughter of a neighbor who lived some distance away. But his first night without the small doll under his roof, he had a very vivid dream. The doll announced that she was the Virgin, Queen of Heaven, and that she belonged there, in his house. She was not to be removed. She further admonished him that if he didn't wish her presence under his roof, he was to destroy the doll.

Waking, he of course thought, *Whoa, weird dream.* But aha! There she was, sitting beside his bed, the very doll he had carried away to his neighbor's place. She had returned, leaving a trail of tiny footprints behind her right up to his front door. He stared into her face and wondered if what he had experienced the night before was indeed a dream—or was it a bona fide vision? *Hmmm, let's see,* he thought. Taking his morning cigarette, he placed the lit end on her cheek. Lo and behold, the doll began to cry. The trace of her tear is still evident on the right cheek of the image lodged above the altar in the shrine. Because, of course, a shrine was inevitable. What else is a peasant to do when the Virgin puts her foot down? Tell the bishop to build a shrine!

This is the Christian interpretation of the Virgin's appearance, and if it sounds as though I tell it tongue-in-cheek, it is not from lack of respect. There are other traditions related to this site that pre-date the years denominated AD. It has been acknowledged as a sacred site, a "miracle-working site" to be specific, by people whose adorations were centered in the earth goddess Coatlicue.

Talpa, a town with a permanent population of about six-thousand, lies cradled at the bottom of a deep valley, a few miles off the two-lane road that wanders through the mountains between Mascota and Guadalajara. Wooded hills surround it on all sides, but the air is clean and clear, laced with the scent of pine trees, orange blossoms, and *palos santos,* those incense-infused strips of wood that smolder and send up clouds of fragrant smoke. The herb vendor who plies his wares in the plaza offers great bunches of dried oregano. But the predominant odor is sweetness—of fruit, simmering in enormous copper *cazuelas* over wood fires. Talpa is famous not only for the Virgin, but for fruits of the earth, fashioned into a vast variety of edible souvenirs. Rows of preserved fruit rolls—guayabas, mangos, apricots and more—are flanked by syrup-filled bottles of whole fruits stuffed with other fruits, or nuts, or who knows what. Cellophane bags of sugar-crusted gumdrop-shaped sweets rest on counters and in the palms of strolling children and adults alike. Ranks of home-bottled *rompope,* a Mexican mixture of eggnog, fruit and tequila, each a distinctive shade of pastel pink, orange or lavender, stand ready to be carried home, a remembrance of Talpa for those left behind.

Thousands of visitors come to Talpa each year, pilgrims who troop through a large concrete arch welcoming them to Talpa, who spend money on Virgin *chatzka* for sale in the main plaza of Talpa, who approach with reverence the church at Talpa, wearing T-shirts inscribed with big bold letters saying "TALPA (fill in the date)." The Virgin of Talpa is a financial bonanza for the town whose name she bears.

Our friend Chano has a whole wardrobe of Talpa T-shirts. He and wife Hilda make the pilgrimage every year. Hilda explained that they go to commemorate her brother who died and left his Dodge van to them. Actually, he died in the van and wasn't found for several days. We think Chano was the only one willing to clean the vehicle out and claim it. But claim it he did, and somehow all this merits a yearly pilgrimage to Talpa.

Hilda and her son by another marriage walk the route beside the pilgrim road. They do it upright with no sticky *nopales* in their knees. Chano and Hilda's mother drive the Dodge van alongside. A few years ago on their way back up the dizzying escarpment dubbed *La Espina del Diablo* (The Devil's Backbone), the van gave up the ghost—or at least the engine. Or maybe it was the clutch. (Much gets lost among three languages, Spanish, English, and car talk.) Chano left it with a local auto mechanic. *Chatzka* dealers are not the only merchants who profit from pilgrims in Talpa.

The square surrounding the massive pink stone shrine with its twin cream-colored towers is a merchandiser's paradise. Everyone wants something to prove they were there, and the town thrives on the commerce. This fact did not escape the notice of the bishop of nearby Mascota a century or two ago. Jealous of prospering Talpa, the Mascota bishop kidnapped the Virgin and installed her in Mascota's own cathedral, claiming that she herself had grown tired of the commercial atmosphere and had run away to his protection. But the very next day she was gone. She had returned to the Shrine of Talpa, leaving a trail of little tiny footprints behind her all the way home.

The museum behind the shrine is a treasure trove of Virgin history and memorabilia. The Virgin has different outfits for different occasions, and you can see her large wardrobe displayed in glass cases. One might wonder who does the dressing and undressing. My friend Roberto's mother used to serve with a group of women who tended to the image of the Virgin of Zapopan near Guadalajara. He told me that his mother would bring him stories about that Virgin leaving tiny muddy footprints around the altar after a heavy rain, so the little lady at Talpa is evidently not the only virgin who gets around. Given Roberto's mother's duties, perhaps the Virgin of Talpa has a similar retinue, a group of ladies who do her laundry and change her underwear. Because there they are on display—little tiny undergarments. One rather cringes to think of burly bishops or priests tending to these tasks—but, well, who knows?

Chief among the exhibits at the museum is a portrait gallery of the formidable line of bishops who have served as protectors of the tiny Virgin over the centuries. To a man they wear don't-mess-with-the-Virgin expressions designed to inspire the fear of, well, if not God, at least of the *Diablo* whose *espina* is the only way out of town. Such a lot of testosterone for one little Virgin! One can't help but wonder if what they're protecting is not the Virgin (Isn't this a case of role reversal? Isn't it the Virgin's job to do the protecting?) but the commerce she generates in the wake of those tiny little footprints.

From the vast array of *agradecimientos* on display throughout the museum, it would seem that the Virgin has had a lot of success in the protection business. The word means "expression of thanks." *Agradecimientos* in this context is artwork—drawings and paintings usually, done in vivid color—depicting everyday situations in which the Virgin has provided a protective presence for those in peril. The ones on display when I was there date back to the 1920s, though I'm assured there are other works stored in the vaults of the shrine that date further back. Just the samples on display provide a rich tapestry of the social and cultural history of Mexico, the ordinary plights and circumstances in which ordinary people find themselves. There are story-pictures of confrontations outside cantinas, school buses hurtling off cliffs, *machete* accidents in cornfields, automobiles careening into each other, suspension bridges collapsing, fishermen struggling in waves, donkey carts overturning, crocodiles attacking children. Okay, ordinary everyday plights if you happen to live in rural Mexico.

But isn't it in ordinary, everyday life where our real pilgrimages take place? Isn't it the daily step by step, putting one foot in front of the other in order to get through the day, washing the dishes, the floors, the babies, and yes, washing the underwear? For pilgrims who show up faithfully every day to perform life's routine tasks, there is no need for *nopalitos*. Let those tasks remain undone, and someone will provide a prod or a poke.

Is routine actually ritual in disguise? One of my favorite books is Kathleen Norris's little gem *The Quotidian Mysteries: Liturgy, Laundry, and "Women's Work."* She compares the daily work that must be done, and redone, and done once again—like laundry and cooking, mending, and cleaning—chores that in the past have traditionally been the province of women—to the rituals performed in churches and in the course of daily worship. It's the little rituals, she says, that keep love alive and the community intact, whether the community is one of family or faith. The morning kiss, the cup of coffee, the laundry done on time. It's the ritual that saves us, that comes to our rescue when things get tense and challenging. It is in times of crisis that the words of prayers uttered perfunctorily day after day flare into beacons of comfort and hope. All of a sudden we're listening

152

and cherishing every word. Ask any widow or widower. What they miss most is the routine that's been disrupted.

So in my foundering around down here in Mexico, talking about "leaving church," I have to consider what exactly it is that I want to leave behind. I'm still working on that. In the meantime, I can rail on about my childhood religious "culture." I can smile indulgently at the "cultural" Catholicism I see around me, poke gentle fun at the Virgin's change of wardrobe. But more times than not, culture provides comfort. It's "comfortable" knowing what to expect, whether it's the well-worn beads of a rosary, or the certain knowledge that the Lord's Prayer comes *here* in the order of service. Rituals are only empty until someone starts tinkering with them.

Our everyday journeys may not involve the physical stress of pilgrimages to Talpa, but they can be just as rigorous in other ways. When I was bouncing around the world on airplanes, I found that landmarks and touchstones were important. It was comforting knowing, for example, that Hampton Inns had soft pillows, a bowl of apples at the reception desk, and eggs on their breakfast buffet. Put me somewhere else, and I was thrown off course. Provided with an essential routine, I could pay attention to what mattered: the presentation and the people who came to hear it.

So, brand new to Virgin Territory, not sure of what mattered any more, I clung to new rituals and routine and settled into a new form of communion. I knew that it mattered that, back from his morning walk with Cody, Larry would ask me if I wanted another cup of coffee. I'd thank him and ask if he wanted breakfast, and he'd respond, "Sounds good." It mattered that the garbage man came on Monday and Friday, that the housekeepers came on those same days, that the market was Thursday, and that breakfast with friends at La Casita was on Tuesday. It mattered that at that breakfast, Irma and Ceci knew I wanted an avocado sandwich with bacon, a side of papaya, and a cup of Abuelita hot cocoa. Call it routine or ritual, when it was put before me, it was a sign someone cared enough to remember.

"Give us this day our daily bread." Mary Baker Eddy interprets these words as: *"Give us grace for today. Feed the famished affections."* Virgin or no Virgin, daily doses of grace and affection beat a T-shirt any time.

154

"GIVE US THIS DAY, OUR DAILY ..."
CHOCOLATE!

I have been guilty, as most gringos have been, to responding to friends' inquiries of "What can we bring you?" with a vociferous, "Chocolate! Good chocolate." It was a matter of consternation to me why, in the country (even before it was a country) that gave chocolate to the Old World, it seems impossible to find a decent chocolate bar. There doesn't seem to be even anything on a par with a Hershey's kiss, which is setting the bar pretty darn low. I have hovered lovingly over gifts of San Francisco Ghirardelli's squares, Suchard and Frigor bars from Switzerland, and bags of Dove kisses purchased at the corner Walgreen's when I go to Lubbock.

But I'm faced with a dilemma when supplied with the genuinely wonderful stuff from colder climates. If I exercise self-restraint, storage is a problem. Put it in the fridge or freezer, and you have to wait for it to warm up. Leave it out at "room temperature," and you've got a foil-wrapped mess. What is a chocolate lover to do without a local source to satisfy that dark-tinged hunger? Then I had chocolate fondue at my friend Karen's, across the *estero*.

"Where did you get this chocolate?" I asked, dunking my second piece of fresh pineapple in a deep dark puddle of almost black chocolate laced with cinnamon, vanilla, and almond flavors. It clung to the fruit with just the right consistency. There were also strawberries on the plate, and they were going even faster than the pineapple, but chocolate tends to run off round things, where if you've got a nice flat surface you can sort of pile it up and get more on.

"At the grocery in town," she answered. "It's those tablets you get in the cardboard cartons, you know the cylindrical ones—Abuelita, Ibarra, Don So-and-So," she ticked off familiar brand names. "I just stick some in the microwave with a little cream and stir. That's it."

That's it? That's all that's required to reach Nirvana? When did life get so simple? Those tablets—and I've seen them for ages in grocery stores in the States, as well as in Mexico—have always been a mystery to me. Right on the label it says, "chocolate for the table." Hard as a table, I concluded, having once bought a carton. About three inches in diameter and half an inch thick, each tablet is sectioned into pie shapes. Try breaking them in pieces, and they shatter. Try to bite one, and you're liable to sacrifice a crown. You probably wouldn't be inclined to bite one, as the tablets are riddled with sugar crystals and other stuff that looks gritty and inedible. This is a product lacking all the charms of chocolate—until you melt it. Ahhhh! Then it gets magical.

There are no paraffin or preservatives in this chocolate. To make a daily cup of cocoa, put some chunks in a teacup with a little water and nuke it for twenty seconds. Whip it with a fork (or an Aerolatte) until the chocolate is totally dissolved and the liquid slightly frothy. Or you could use one of those wooden rattle-looking things specifically designed for this purpose by the Aztecs. Pity they didn't have microwaves, right? Add more water or milk almost to the brim, zap some more and ta dah! Hot chocolate! To make *champurado*, stir some Maizena—basically cornstarch—into the first stage. The mixture will thicken into *champurado*—what Mexicans think of first when they think hot chocolate.

However it's prepared, Mexican chocolate a'la Abuelita is a daily ritual. Thanks, "little grandmother," for making me feel more at home.

CHAPTER 14

X MARKS
THE SPOT

Say ye to the daughter of Zion, Behold, thy salvation cometh,
And thou shalt be called, Sought out, a city not forsaken.
Isaiah

"La Peñita needs a miracle. What we need is a Virgin-sighting, like in Talpa, something that would draw pilgrims and tourists."

Luis talks as if he's joking, but I think he may be serious. He and I are having Thursday morning breakfast at Xaltemba, a restaurant that is an art gallery—or vice-versa. Luis is one of those elegant older Mexican men who command attention by demeanor more than anything else. But Luis also looks good. His shock of thick white hair matches the umbrellas erected against a cobalt blue December sky and the linen tablecloth spread between us. From over the wall outside in the main plaza, we can hear the *tianguis* in full swing. Vendors hawk their wares, and an African drum group is busy annoying the clientele at Soley's just around the corner. Soley's, with its umbrellas out front and its tables set right on the cobble-stoned street, gives you a front row seat to the market in the main plaza and all that goes on there. Xaltemba is where you retreat for conversation.

Luis publishes a bi-monthly "guide" to the Riviera Nayarit, which is mainly a vehicle for local advertisers. He wants my perspective as a newcomer. La Peñita always presents him with a challenge. There's only so much you can say about the Thursday market.

"We need a miracle," he repeats. "In more ways than one."

How many times had I thought the same thing about the string of towns scattered across West Texas that I'd lived in? The first thirty years of my life plus a few more had been spent longing for some sort of magic that would transform the agrarian monotony surrounding me to an urban wonderland of glitterati and literati. My heart yearned for art openings, cultural events, poetry readings, standup comedy acts, performance art— something, anything, other than a rehash of Friday night's high school football game or plans for Sunday afternoon watching the Dallas Cowboys. I longed for "real" conversation with other people besides my family, but rarely did I find anyone willing to take me seriously, or even humorously. Eyes would either shift or glaze over if I launched into a description of what I might have read recently. I was an NPR fan waiting in the wings. Neither did anybody seem to "get" what I thought was really funny. If talking to yourself is scary to other people, laughing to yourself is downright sinister.

We did converse around the Jackson dinner table, though the "rehashing" there generally centered on politics, the dangers of creeping socialism, and the perils posed by the Tri-Lateral Commission and its plans for one-world government. When we laughed—and we did quite often—the standard for laughter was usually set by my father's taste, somewhere along the lines of Red Skelton and the Three Stooges. Our family has always known how to have fun with food, especially if it's in the air or on someone's face.

Dad also thought Art Buchwald and James Thurber were funny, and I read and re-read collections of their columns we had on the bookshelf, trying to hone my conversational gambits to what I considered the same razor sharp irony. I did not enjoy great success. The humor of middle-aged men doesn't translate well when delivered by an adolescent young woman. But the only model I had for being a funny female was Lucille Ball. I found her irritating and manipulative, definitely not someone I'd want to sit down with and talk. I was delighted with Cornelia Otis Skinner, but it would be years before I discovered Dorothy Parker. Lily Tomlin was not even a glimmer on the skyline.

I longed for a skyline, something like the line drawing of Manhattan, which served as a banner across "The Talk of the Town" in outdated copies of *The New Yorker* that I culled through at the McGee's when I babysat for them across the street. In my mind's eye, I'd superimpose that magazine image over the three tall buildings that comprised the Lubbock skyline, visible one mile east across a bare cotton field at the end of our block. I knew that someday I'd live in a place with an honest-to-goodness skyline, not one I had to semi-imagine. I'd be surrounded by interesting people who were adept in a wide variety of subjects, people who would "get" me and laugh at what I thought was funny. Then, after thirty-three years, I moved with Larry to "L.A."

Well, it wasn't actually Los Angeles, though from mid-continent I really didn't know the difference. I knew there was a huge glob of population out there on the West Coast, and as far as I was concerned, that was L.A.

"Don't go out to California and get all weird on us," admonished friend after friend, speaking in that distinctive accent accomplished by never moving the lower jaw. I'd smile sweetly and shrug. I so wanted weird. Maybe I would have gotten authentic weird if we'd actually moved to L.A. Where we really moved was to Orange County—south Orange County. There was no skyline, little literati, and the glitterati that occasionally breached "The Orange Curtain" arrived behind tinted windows of stretch limos that sped down Pacific Coast Highway and slithered into gate-guarded communities and resorts.

There were, however, many more opportunities to attend cultural events, theater productions, concerts, and all that I'd longed for. The Sunday Calendar Section of the *Los Angeles Times* replaced for me the outdated copies of *The New Yorker* I'd treasured in my youth. Here I was, within driving range of actual Broadway productions, art openings, author signings, and any other number of cultural attractions. It was only that the outlay of time and money to take advantage of all those things was often prohibitive. So "culture" was replaced with outdoor activities, walks at the marina, watching Larry's surf sessions in the morning, volleyball in the sand, and beach fires at night. All this took place in an environment where both bodies and landscapes were well manicured and meticulously groomed. Such vulgar activities as filling your car with gas and having it washed were often scrupulously screened from public view by carefully tended vegetation as foreign and as transplanted as the labor crew performing those services.

La Peñita, Mexico, is very different in this regard. Here every potential service is offered every potential customer, and details of that service are inscribed in multi-colored signage on every available surface of every available wall. They'll balance your tires, mix your concrete, and give your chicken a bath right there, street side. Emerging from a lush jungle and entering La Peñita's sphere of influence along Highway 200 is an assault on the senses. If you don't have business there (but you probably do), you would never feel inclined to stop, pull to one side, and say, "Oh my, this looks charming and inviting. Why don't we spend some time here!"

La Peñita is such an un-charming town that the glamour-conscious folks who are promoting Riviera Nayarit constantly leave it off the maps they print for tourists, including, instead, much smaller villages like Chacala, San Francisco (known locally as San Pancho), Sayulita, and Guayabitos. Admittedly each of those small towns has its own distinct charm. They all possess that certain come-hither attitude, with one eye always winking toward the tourist trade. La Peñita is like the awkward older sister whom no one wants to marry. It's she who runs the errands, does the cooking, works behind the scenes, has loads of children, and carries out the garbage. She never quite has time to put herself together. Like the woman whose work is never done, the town always looks unfinished, something always in a state of construction or repair. Among the colored walls—and Los Peñitanos are not shy about the rainbow of shades they use for painting their walls—you can always find bare cinderblock walls adorned at the top with sprouts of

161

wilting rebar. Our friend Regino explains, "Six and a half days a week I work for someone else. On Saturday afternoon I buy cinderblock and cement. On Sunday I build on my house. No mortgage, but it's mine." The unspoken accusation hangs in the air. He's too polite to say what others have voiced: "We're in this economic mess because of Americans and their great big mortgages."

Whether the opinion is true or not, Mexicans are always impressed with the amount of debt they hear that Americans carry. Credit is practically non-existent for the majority of citizens here, especially for hard assets like a car or a house. Only the very rich have credit cards, and obtaining one of those through a Mexican bank involves as much documentation as applying for a home loan in the United States. Maybe more.

There are, however, funds available for those who want to start small businesses. These loans are made locally by people who know the people involved, and they are scrupulously repaid monthly and even weekly, out of the receipts from the enterprise. Loans go to those who have a known track record for diligence, sobriety, and hard work, who aren't inclined to get up and move somewhere else overnight, so it's no wonder that many businesses are run by women with children. Cruise up and down the main avenida. Read the names. See the faces. There are so many women's businesses, I can't begin to list them all—Lorena's, Juanita's, Adriana's, Lupita's, Wendy's, Daisy's, Rocio's, Angye's. Near the best jewelry shop in town, find the "chicken ladies," whose tiny shops consist of little more than a small table on which are spread a few carcasses of freshly slaughtered birds, the relatives of whom are squawking in the interior courtyard behind. As far as local entrepreneurship goes, women are the oil in the engine.

That engine runs beneath a battered exterior. La Peñita has never fully recovered from the ravages of 2002's Hurricane Kenna. The pair of seahorse sculptures that once marked the entrance to a *malecón* now precide over a jumble of fishing boats and equipment drawn up on the strip of narrow beach that remains. Kenna slammed smack dab into the Nayarit coast with winds of 140 miles per hour. It took a huge bite out of this particular stretch of Jaltemba Bay beachfront. Neighboring Guayabitos was left with the broad sweeping playgrounds of sand and gentle water that attract tourists, but in La Peñita the ocean now comes in as shore break, sometimes still spilling over into the village streets. Some blame the jetty where sits my Virgin. Whatever the cause, La Peñita's beachfront is disappointing. Silent abandoned buildings sit in decay along the oceanfront, belying the bustling market town and fishing village that stretches only blocks behind.

For La Peñita is the place where people shop. No hurricane has changed that fact. They go there to get keys made, their oil changed, their nails done. They buy brooms, cleaning supplies, coffins, carbon paper (one sheet at a time, if you please), and giant loaves of Bimbo white bread. The few stores along the main avenue that do cater to tourist tastes are not galleries, or specialty dress shops, or even government-sponsored outlets for local artisans. Instead they sell stuff that little kids can afford to give each other or merchandise for adults with a taste for ashtrays made from seashells, and luridly dyed beachwear. La Peñita is a working class town that hasn't been gentrified.

But like Soho and Taos used to be, it is a place where artists and writers can actually afford to live. More and more are making their homes here, welcomed specifically as a particular class by Mexican immigration authorities. (Other welcomed groups are retired couples and women over fifty years old. The last group is not required to take a blood test for AIDS to obtain legal status. I don't want to explore the reasoning behind that stance—I think it might be insulting.)

One of my favorite artists in La Peñita is Roberto Gil de Montes. "I'm remodeling La Peñita one house at a time," he says. Having lived here almost thirty years, he is gradually making progress. Not too many living painters have work hanging in the Smithsonian. Roberto does. An escapee from Los Angeles, he lives and works in La Peñita, periodically buying a new house, renovating it and/or building a studio, and then moving on to the next project. At any given time he and his partner of over thirty years, Eddie Dominguez, own two or three homes in various states of construction. "They're also good to put guests in," says Roberto. "That way we don't have to have them underfoot."

That's good because Roberto and Eddie are busy people, usually either welcoming guests or planning for their arrival. Eddie, a former general manager for the Telemundo network in both Los Angeles and San Francisco, is inclined to think that if he doesn't have four projects going at once, he's slacking off. Roberto, with his eye for aesthetics and attention to detail, is good at carrying many of Eddie's concepts through to perfection. Xaltemba Gallery and Restaurant, where Luis and I are having breakfast, is one of their projects. It's made a huge difference in our frumpy little town.

It was a grimy shell of a building just off the main plaza, perhaps one of Kenna's victims, but Roberto and Eddie saw its potential. They installed a creative chef in the kitchen ("Food is art, too!" insists Roberto), and invested in paint. A mustard-yellow wall came to define one side of the patio dining area on the main floor. It provides a vibrant backdrop for guest performances of live music, regional dances and late night cabaret acts. On evenings when there are no live artists on hand, on an adjacent pure white wall two stories high, Eddie projects a variety of international silver screen memorabilia. Flickering YouTube images of screen goddesses from the past light up the night. Rita Hayworth tosses her hair back, sings and vamps to "Put the Blame on Mame." Dalida belts out "Torna a Surriento" with a view of Vesuvius in the background, and Marilyn Monroe revels in Tiffany gems and gentlemen while singing "Diamonds Are a Girl's Best Friend." As the night wears on and the Mexican dinner crowd arrives, the cast on the wall shifts to Latin luminaries Lucha Villa, Lola Beltrán, and Amalia Mendoza. There is always music, but never enough to drown out conversation and camaraderie.

Off the main patio a series of arches define the entry to the art gallery and the more intimate table settings inside. Roberto hauled back from San Francisco an ornate Chinese opium bed and reassembled it as a bar near the main entrance. Its dark wood glistens against a deep red wall, providing a welcome focus for clientele that wander in from the tables set up for smokers on the cobblestone street outside. Conversation ebbs and flows, Cuban and Mexican Spanish, British and American English, and French from Canada and Belgium for the most part, but there's usually an Italian or two hanging about, as well.

Around a corner and up a tiled staircase there is a cozy but ample space for more exhibits, a mingling room for regular openings and artist receptions. The furniture is comfortable and invites conversation, but most important, for me, is the chaise lounge and lectern provided for presentations by poets and authors. It was here that early drafts of *Virgin Territory* were first exposed to public scrutiny. Roberto pressed me to share, and on the Virgin's day in 2008, with fireworks going off in the plaza outside and a real live audience before me, I opened my mouth and read what was then Chapter Three. Gosh darn it, people laughed where they were supposed to and cried in places where I bared my soul! It was one of the most validating experiences I'd ever had. I swore then and there that I'd finish the thing come hell, high water, or another hurricane.

This all comes rushing back as Luis talks of La Peñita's need for a miracle. "Pirates!" he exclaims with inspiration. "Surely there were pirates in this bay. Maybe they buried treasure and left a map. You know, 'X marks the spot.'" He laughs and rises to say goodbye.

I settle back into the round pigskin-covered *equipale* chair and stroke the white table cloth.

"Otro café?" offers Genaro, one of Roberto's several godsons waiting tables.

"Por supuesto! Gracias," I answer, grateful to have a few moments of reflection. Xaltemba, I've come to realize, is everything I ever longed for in the way of culture when I was growing up in

West Texas. Here it is, in rude and unpolished authenticity, far from any population center, located in a humble *pueblo* devoid of any skyline. I couldn't be happier anywhere else. Ugly older sister La Peñita has won my love. I already have my miracle right here.

POWER CORD

Antiquity is charming except where electricity is concerned. When the house on Golondrinas was first constructed, the builders failed to avail themselves of that particular modern-day miracle. When electricity was added later, it was done in a creative manner, even for Mexico. But our most recent power failure was out in the street: CFE's problem to fix, ours to endure. We spent a summer Saturday anxiously waiting for help, not willing to think of not having relief until Monday. Government agencies— and the electric company in Mexico is a federal agency—do not work on Sundays.

Life seems to go out of a house when the refrigerator stands stoically silent, the fans overhead freeze in mid-air, and after a thoughtless flush, there is no responding water pump action bringing *agua* from the *aljibe* below. Repeated calls to the company bring the response, *"Ratito, ratito."* Soon, soon, we're promised. My sense of "powerlessness" grows.

"I drew them with cords of a man, with bands of love," Hosea quotes Jehovah, describing the close bond between Creator and created. I picture a Tool Time Deity covered in sockets, each of us with a power cord to plug in. But the Hebrew word *chebel*, translated in the King James Bible as "cords of a man," means something else entirely. A *chebel* is an *umbilical* cord. Follow that kind of cord to its source and you won't find a Guy God, even one in touch with His feminine side. The power source at the end of a *chebel* is Mother God, Creatress, Nurturer. She is the Almighty, which comes from El Shaddai—"the breasted one."

The very nature of an umbilical cord brings oneness, Mother and child inseparable. The child is totally dependent, yes, but never powerless. "Great with child," is a power-filled image. I settle into these thoughts as I wait for the electric company, the heavy humid air of mid-summer closing in around me. I wait, and wait longer, reminding myself that patience, after all, is a quality imposed on pregnancy. The final outcome is inevitable, and it will happen when the time is right.

The work crew arrives long after sunset, just as we've finished foraging in the pantry for dinner, and decided to strip off and bathe in the pool. Many apologies. *"Muchas emergencias,"* they explain. I continue to pray as, weary and wet with sweat, they poke and fiddle with live wires in the dark. One man is charged with holding a wobbly and a waning flashlight on the job at hand. I can't bear to watch. I stay inside and hold a mental image of each of them connected by a *chebel* of love to Mother Life. I shut out the picture of a crispy-fried CFE crew on the sidewalk.

But within an hour the lights come on. Luz! We have power!

Funny, I think later. Remember, the Spanish term for "to give birth" is *dar a luz*—to give to the light. But that involves cutting the cord. *There's got to be a metaphor there somewhere,* I think. For now, I'm grateful I can finally open the refrigerator, indulge in ice cubes, take a shower, and go to bed. I slide into clean-and-cool-sheet sleep under the comforting hum of an air conditioner.

CHAPTER 15

AND THE WOMAN
FLED INTO THE
WILDERNESS

WILDERNESS. Loneliness; doubt; darkness.
Spontaneity of thought and idea; the vestibule in which
a material sense of things disappears, and spiritual sense
unfolds the great facts of existence.
Mary Baker Eddy, "Glossary," *Science and Health*

The road from Guayabitos to Tepic is a two-lane asphalt ribbon that snakes upward from sea level to over 3,000 feet. There's a surprise around every turn—a gash of blue Pacific framed by jungle, a colorful shrine to Guadalupe on a hair pin curve, or an up-ended Corona beer truck, its spilled cargo waiting the scavenging motorists who abandon vehicles in mid-lane in order to join the "rescue" efforts.

On this particular trip, my eyes are fixed on the digital compass readout located on the rearview mirror of Hummercita. Tepic, the capital of the State of Nayarit, is in the throes of vast road construction projects with *deviación* signs posted one after another. The last few trips, there have been so many detours that when we've finally entered the city, it's been from a totally unexpected direction. I'm determined not to get turned around this time. I want to keep track of the road I'm on. Larry is driving, so it's easy for me to look at the compass. We are still an hour away from the city and so far it has registered each of the eight directions: N, NE, E, SE, S, SW, W, NW, lingering mostly in the N, NE sector. *It's a good thing we know where we'll eventually end up*, I think, glancing down at the map I'm holding. *Sometimes it feels as if we're going backwards.*

The trip that day in October 2009, seemed like one big metaphor for my life. Since moving to Mexico three years before, my personal compass had made as many gyrations as Hummercita's. For someone "who didn't go to doctors," who had invested so much of life being a Christian Scientist in a very public way, I now was spending an inordinate amount of time taking painkillers and talking to physicians and surgeons. I was headed now to Tepic for one more surgery, relieved that something was finally being done about the intense pain I'd been experiencing. How had I ended up like this?

Perhaps I'd embarked on my "road to Tepic" even before I'd moved to Mexico. Lying awake over the past months, I'd finally had opportunity to reflect on a life that, in its early years, had seemed easy going and straightforward. The main thing in those early years was to be a "good" Christian Scientist, show up for church twice a week, and everything else would take care of itself. For the most part it did. I read the daily Bible lesson, followed the rules, and never felt inclined to trouble myself much about "the road not taken."

I started thinking differently after I'd been in jail a while. As a county jail chaplain, I had heard stories that reached beyond the ken of my privileged and protected suburban life. I began developing something my husband always said I lacked—facial poise. It is an essential trait for anyone to whom others bare their souls. I see it epitomized now in Guadalupe's countenance—the downcast eyes, the attitude of listening, the non-judgmental bearing. Somehow I knew instinctively that was the demeanor to adopt when sitting with inmates on those hard metal stools in rooms that smelled of disinfectant. I would never have identified myself with Mary back then, would have felt uncomfortable with the comparison. Could it be possible, though, that anyone who longs to respond to others' troubles, listening to them with a God-gifted heart, naturally reflects that spiritual ideal? Through those encounters with inmates, I discovered many things about myself and about my own potential for loving. I came to value my times in jail as much as the weekly church services in suburbia. Maybe more. I still showed up on Sunday mornings, but I was pretty sure that if any of my new acquaintances had tagged along with me, we wouldn't have been invited out to brunch.

I liked going to brunch, though. It was good to be with church-women talking frankly. My friends did not have quiet demeanors. They had plans. This was a group who was ready to change the world, and we discussed projects over morning coffee and lunches at the marina. What we didn't discuss was "the change" looming on all our horizons. We were into metaphysics, not menopause. Or maybe those conversations took place when I wasn't around. Not having children myself, I tended to zone out when the subject of prom dresses and orthodontia came up. Maybe I missed the communal conversation about growing older.

Actually, I tended to dismiss the subject of age altogether. I was on a roll, Baby. By 1994, I was traveling all over California, supporting other chaplains and giving training sessions. By 1996, I was traveling the country, spending almost a third of my days away from home. If there were any major *ta dah* announcement (i.e., "Attention! Your body is now going through a major life transition"), I never heard it. I just kept going and going and going, wondering who kept turning up the thermostat. I even forgot my fiftieth birthday until the customs agent in the Prague airport, looking at my passport, wished me "Hoppy Burday" when I arrived for a three-night stay in the Czech Republic late in July 1999. That was a marathon summer. I'd left John Wayne Airport the afternoon of July Fourth. I didn't come back home again for six weeks, filling speaking engagements and training sessions in Boston, New York, England, Switzerland, the Czech Republic, and then back to New York once more. I arrived home exhausted, and left two days later. Larry had planned a surprise trip to Cabo San Lucas to celebrate our thirtieth anniversary. I probably would have forgotten that, too, at the rate I was going.

So it continued, through the 2000 calendar rollover, the events of 9/11, and into 2003. Public attitudes towards religion and spirituality were undergoing tectonic shifts. No longer were these topics *verboten* in polite society; they were the currency of common conversation. It thrilled me to be in on that conversation. The venues where I spoke varied from bookstores to bistros, medical conferences on palliative care to juvenile detention centers, Catholic support groups to Pentecostal prayer meetings, training sessions for AIDS hospice workers to women's studies seminars. I felt fully in tune with my work and my colleagues. It was a new millennium and the world was changing before our eyes.

But with the invasion of Iraq, a different kind of change swept the country. The mental atmosphere seemed to congeal into a spirit of self-righteous rage and retribution. There was a change in the church that employed me, as well. It might be termed reactionary, that collective shift in thought to an "Us vs. Them" posture. As the U.S. Department of Homeland Security shifted into high gear, so did the church administration. No longer, as speakers, were we encouraged to be open and spontaneous with our public interactions. We were to submit scripted remarks, and they would be tweaked. Differences rather than similarities were to be emphasized.

I complied in practice, but not in spirit. Sleepless nights were filled with conversations held in my head, in which I'd try to convince those "in charge" that a bunker mentality or an adversarial attitude was far from productive. I didn't deflect the currents of thought swirling around me; I let them suck me in and make me angry. In effect I created my own personal "war zone." It should have come as no surprise then, that I began sustaining actual injuries—a twisted ankle, a dislocated shoulder, knocks on the head. It seemed something or other always had me limping through my duties.

Through it all Larry was my anchor, my safe place to be, the only one with whom I felt free to express myself. But, he, too, was feeling frustrated and discouraged, cut off from his friends at San Onofre beach. Morning discussions there now centered on all-out support for the war. So close to Camp Pendleton and the military facilities at San Diego, any whisper of dissent was regarded as no less than treasonous. Together Larry and I quietly pinned our hopes on the outcome of the 2004 election, hoping our "treasonous" attitude might be vindicated by other parts of America.

It was not to be. I was stunned by the results. Deep inside me I longed to run away, to be alone with God and get things straightened out. But as I've said before, I was having a few problems with "Him," as well.

I continued work through the end of 2004, but in January 2005, I wrote to the church officials asking not to be considered when appointments were made for the speakers bureau the following June. No one responded to that request. Perhaps they thought it presumptuous of me, but I needed to make my break "official," if only to myself. It made my spring schedule bearable, knowing there was an end in sight. I looked forward to a summer and fall when I could kick back, take it easy, and just be. I cleaned out my closets. We took some trips, started fantasizing about retirement—someday.

Then in December 2005, Clark Foam, supplier of over 95% of surfboard blanks in the world, closed its doors for good. It sent the surfboard industry into a tailspin. As a surfboard shaper, Larry no longer had anything to shape. Both of us were now suspended, no plans, no prospects. That's when we took that fateful vacation, bought the house in Mexico, and moved far, far away.

WORDS OF
THE VIRGIN OF GUADALUPE
TO JUAN DIEGO

Listen,

put it into your heart, that what frightened you,

what afflicted you,

is nothing;

do not let it disturb your face, your heart;

do not fear this sickness

nor any other sickness,

nor any sharp and hurtful thing.

Am I not here,

I who have the honor to be your Mother?

Are you not in my shadow and under my protection?

Am I not the source of your joy?

Are you not in the hollow of my mantle,

in the crossing of my arms?

Do you need something more?

CHAPTER 16

"THERE WILL BE AN ANSWER"

When I find myself in times of trouble, Mother Mary comes to me,
Speaking words of wisdom: Let it be. Let it be.
John Lennon and Paul McCartney

I hadn't been conscious of it, but evidently, hidden deep inside me was the idea that someday, somehow, if there was something that wasn't healed or alleviated with Christian Science treatment, I could find a doctor who would "fix" it, even if the solution were only temporary, something that would work until I got my metaphysical act together. After all, hadn't Mary Baker Eddy herself made provision for just such a circumstance right there in *Science and Health?*

> If Christian Scientists ever fail to receive aid from other Scientists,—their brethren upon whom they may call,—God will still guide them into the right use of temporary and eternal means. Step by step will those who trust Him find that "God is our refuge and strength, a very present help in trouble."

It wasn't anyone's fault but my own. I'd forgotten how to "receive aid." Being angry is a tight, hard place to be in, and while I saw myself as a free thinker, "stepping out of the box" of denomination, stepping away from religion of any kind, I'd stepped into something even more constricting. I'd forgotten how to be loved. I needed to learn that all over again. So, while I felt myself cut off from church, country, and family, I turned to a new set of friends and neighbors. I turned, also, to a group of people I'd had little or nothing to do with at any time previous in my life—medical professionals.

The first time I ever visited a hospital as a patient was when I practically crawled into Amerimed Hospital in Puerto Vallarta. Dr. Marquez treated me with gentleness and patience, and not a little bit of wonderment. Here I was a fifty-seven year old woman who had never had a blood test, never taken a pill, and the last shot I'd had was for small pox when I'd entered first grade. He looked at me like I'd dropped from another planet. I acted like I'd come from there. I was terrified of the blood test, and later of being punctured by the IV. With the low blood count I had, I wasn't thinking clearly enough to even reason my way through the ordeal. I did not acquit myself well in the courage department. I smile with gratitude now, thinking of the quiet sense of authority those nurses in their immaculately starched, crisp white uniforms exuded, how their well modulated voices engaged me in conversation to distract me from what was going on with needles and bags of blood suspended overhead.

I have no idea how many physicians came trooping through my room or were involved in that first adventure in surgery. I think it was a colonoscopy, but mercifully I was unconscious. I wasn't unconscious for a later series of X-rays taken in conjunction with a barium enema, but I wish I had been. Maybe it was my age and lack of medical care experience, or the fact that I'm almost six feet tall with blue eyes and platinum hair, but evidently I became a known entity in the Puerto Vallarta medical community. For months after my Amerimed debut, total strangers would greet me, introducing themselves as physicians who had attended me. I was impressed they would remember my face; that's not where their attention would have been focused during the course of their care.

I'd never had much contact even socially with physicians back in the States. They had been neighbors, but were rarely seen, except backing in and out of garages using automatic door openers. Now Dr. Marquez, Fernando, was my friend on Facebook, and I had a roster of other doctors' phone numbers lodged on the memory card of my cell phone. "Here's my card, and that's my cell number," each had said. "Call me if there's any problem, or even if you just have a question." When I did, they were always courteous, assuring me that, yes, I'd done the right thing in calling.

I missed that kind of attention when I found myself in Lubbock the summer of 2007. Larry and I intended spending July and August traveling the western United States, visiting friends we hadn't seen since our move ten months before. We went first to Texas, in order to see Mom. We never hit the road after that. I simply wasn't able to go on. I was bleeding again. It started when we crossed the U.S. border and got worse as we approached Lubbock. We hunkered down at Mom's house, trusting I would improve enough to resume our trip. It didn't happen.

What was it about crossing that border? I was certain, and this would be understandable given my upbringing, that the whole physical situation, this rebellious bleeding body of mine, was purely a mental construct. "You're stressed," Dr. Marquez had told me. I heard it from him and one physician after another. It was no help that I felt I was entering hostile territory when we crossed the border to Texas. It had to do with country, family, and church. I was at odds with them all. But being aware of that fact didn't make the circumstances any better. In fact, it made them worse. I alternated between feeling victimized and persecuted, and then being generally ticked off that I couldn't get my head on straight, couldn't make myself love 'those idiots,' whatever their relation to me. Neither mental state was helpful for any kind of healing, medical or spiritual. As a consequence, the bleeding got worse and I got weaker. I needed to do something to stop it, and I needed to do it quickly.

Even though I'd resorted to doctors and hospitals in Mexico, I wasn't ready to surrender myself to medical care in the United States. It seemed scary. The environment at the Dallas hospital where Mom had been admitted during an emergency the previous fall impressed me as chaotic and unorganized. I couldn't tell nurses and staff from visitors because everyone was so informally dressed, and, while it may have just been the Texas accents, the noise level was almost unbearable. Back at her home, Mom had to call weeks in advance to get an appointment with her primary care physician, and the prescription medicines she was taking seemed to multiply rather than diminish.

You go with what you trust until it doesn't work for you anymore. It had been a major leap of faith for me to jump from Christian Science treatment and check into Amerimed. I wasn't ready to jump from medicine in Mexico to medicine in the United States. I also knew it would be a serious strain on our finances. Mom had Medicare. Larry and I had nothing in the way of health insurance.

We returned to Mexico, making the trip home in record time. I called the doctor's cell phone the evening we arrived, and the next morning I was installed in a private room at Amerimed. My blood count was even lower than when I had been admitted the previous October. It was 3.2, and I needed five units of blood to bring me back to normal.

I wasn't only using Amerimed like a Pemex station: drive 'er in and fill 'er up. They also took out some impressive hemorrhoids in the course of my eleven-day stay there. "There are a few more," the surgeon advised, but he was concerned about causing excessive scar tissue. I was concerned about being normal again. After they put me on my feet again, I set about reclaiming my life.

Two years later in 2009, I recognized the old symptoms—bloating and bleeding, becoming woozy and wobbly while climbing the stairs to the front door. But I ignored them and powered on. I had a mission: finish *Virgin Territory*. I was practically there. Completing the memoir that I'd begun as a blog was cathartic. So much was resolved when recognized and put down on paper. I'd come, I thought, to terms with the resentment and anger I'd felt from my family, had even spent two weeks with them earlier in the summer. Obama had been elected, but I'd basically given up pinning my happiness to the results of a national election. It was the daily interaction with friends and neighbors that mattered. Even the personal financial losses we'd sustained in the economic crisis hadn't kept me from sleeping soundly. *All is right with the world,* I assured myself. *I just need to get out of the house once the heat lets up—start exercising some more.* I put the final period on the last paragraph of the book's first draft, typed a row of asterisks across the bottom, sent it to my editor Laura, and waited for a well-earned *bravo.*

Whew, August was hot! As I settled in to wait for word from Laura, I noticed I wasn't feeling better. I hurt. Now that I wasn't writing, it became more obvious. *Rats. I don't have time for this!* I thought. Foot tapping was going on in my brain. *Okay, Laura, I'm waiting!*

But when I heard from her about that draft, she said, "It feels unfinished." Not what I wanted to hear. "I have the feeling you're not being totally honest," she continued, "like you're avoiding something."

"Oh, really?" I responded. "Whatever do you mean?"

Okay, it was true. What good was a book about finding health and peace in Mexico when evidently I hadn't? I was still hurting. Damn bleeding. Damn body. Damn. Damn. Damn. I set the manuscript aside. I could no longer hold onto a thought long enough to get it onto paper, anyway. Nothing seemed to matter anymore. I settled into a career of playing Bejeweled Blitz online. And kept bleeding.

I went back to my friend, Dr. Marquez, who referred me to a specialist, one with a thick Latino accent. "Of course you cannot concentrate!" the specialist exclaimed during our visit as he looked at the results of another blood test. "You're depressed. It's because you're anemic. You can't focus." He pronounced "focus" as if both vowels were "U"s—like the "U" in *duck*.

"Yep," Larry agreed dryly, imitating the doctor's pronunciation. "It's been pretty hard to 'focus' these days."

"So, can I get some blood?" I asked, swatting at Larry. It was my Pemex fill-up time again. Just give me some blood, and I'd be good to go. But evidently a hemoglobin count of 8.1, though pretty bad, isn't low enough to warrant a transfusion. The doctor suggested iron shots, and he wanted to run more tests to see what was causing the loss of blood.

"There's something right at the base of my spine, up inside," I informed him. "It's like a cattle prod. The pain is intense. It builds up and builds up until I explode and lose a lot of blood. I think it's those hemorrhoids they didn't get the first time."

"Shall I examine you?" he asked. I went behind the privacy screen in his office and began to undress. "Oh, that's not necessary." He seemed alarmed that I would be willing to shed my clothes so readily. "Sit here," he said, and I perched decorously on the examination table he patted. He looked in my eyes. He listened to my heart. He poked around on my backbone, poked at places around my belly, bent my legs, bent my arms. "Does this hurt? Does this? How about this?" He poked everywhere but where I told him the problem was. I wondered what the purpose of all this was, but he was supposed to be the expert. Maybe everything was connected some way, and he'd eventually come up with a valid reason for the pain. He went back to the desk, and I sat down again beside Larry across from him. My modesty was intact, if not my confidence. He looked at me and grew serious.

185

"Maybe you should see a psychiatrist," he suggested.

For days, no, weeks, I had been emotionally on edge, avoiding friends, avoiding anyone. If someone asked the simple question, "How are you?" I'd dissolve in tears. Dishes slipped from my fingers and I'd forget what I was going to do before I even lifted my body out of a chair—so why make the effort? I couldn't read. I couldn't think. I couldn't even sit through a thirty-minute sitcom on television. Finishing sentences required a major effort, and if I did succeed, the result was rarely civil. The only thing I felt capable of was sitting for hours playing one minute Bejeweled Blitz. Swapping out the digital gems, watching them cascade and disappear in crackling explosions, I felt like I was accomplishing something. I'd do *this*, and *that* would happen. Wasn't that progress?

No. It was mesmeric. I was losing mental as well as physical control, but I no longer could distinguish which was cause and which was effect. All my training and background gave me to believe that the mental governed the physical, not vice-versa. But my mental capacities were in shreds. I was depending on finding a physical cause to be righted so I could get back to being Susan once more. See a psychiatrist? Larry and I looked at each other, then broke down in helpless desperate laughter. Talk about "square one." It seemed he'd sent me straight back there.

"Are you saying this is all in my head?" I finally got out.

"No, not at all," he assured me. "It's not in your head. But a psychiatrist can help you deal with the depression caused by the pain."

He was serious. He looked genuinely concerned. But I was now genuinely angry.

"Why not," I snarled through clenched teeth, "get rid of the blankety-blanking pain, and then I won't be depressed." Only I didn't say "blankety-blanking." I couldn't help it. That "focus" word was still in my head.

He lifted his eyebrows and then shrugged. "I'm prescribing a colonoscopy. Maybe they'll find something." We were done.

But they didn't find anything with the colonoscopy. At least nothing they told me about, nothing they said needed attention, or could possibly be causing me pain and bleeding. In retrospect, I honestly don't know how hard they looked, or where they looked. People tend to see what they expect to see. The surgeon who had operated on me two years before was the same one who did this colonoscopy. Perhaps he simply expected to see the excellent results of his previous work.

In Mexico, every person is responsible for his own medical records. You yourself carry them around from one doctor or hospital to another. I had a growing pile. They sent me off with a DVD to add to it and a few snap shots of my interior. They also gave me a small glass vial with something floating in it. No explanation. No instructions. I didn't watch the DVD. I set the vial down in a desk drawer, wondering what the heck I was supposed to do with it. And life went on—painfully. *So much for "temporary means,"* I thought, remembering the Christian Science term for physical methods of healing.

Maybe it was all in my head. I no longer trusted my judgment or anyone else's. Where was all that tender care I'd come to expect from Mexican doctors, the quiet competency, the there-for-you follow up? If my problem hadn't been resolved with Christian Science, and now the doctors couldn't find anything, what in heaven's name was I supposed to do?

A week or so later, I drove my friend Marilyn back to her house after an outing. Pulling up at the curb, I lost control and began sobbing into Hummercita's steering wheel. When I could speak I poured out what I was feeling. "I hate this. I hate dealing with all this flesh and body stuff. I've betrayed everything I've been taught, everything I've lived by, and for what? I don't know what's wrong with me. No one knows. I've always thought of myself as a dancing column of light," I wailed. "I don't know what I am anymore."

Marilyn was patient and comforting. In her past life she had been administrator of a clinic employing thirty-five doctors and ninety-two other employees. She was the ideal hand-holder for me, knowledgeable about medical processes, but under no illusions as to the omniscience of medical practitioners. "Don't put up with crazy doctors," she now counseled me. "You don't need crazy in your life. But you do need some practical help. You need blood in your body just like you need food." She smiled at me. "Get your blood count up. Then you can get back to being a dancing column of light."

"Iron shots," the doctor with the accent had suggested. No one would give me a transfusion, so I decided to follow his advice. Not wanting to make the long trip into Puerto Vallarta every other day or so, I consulted Dr. Lidiana who lived halfway up the hill on a really bad cobblestone road in La Peñita. *La doctora* possessed a serene Madonna expression, radiant skin, and compassionate brown eyes. She looked intently into my blue ones, her brows coming slightly together as she listened quietly and attentively. The whole of her demeanor was that of one who gave herself totally to healing. *If ever there were a window to heaven,* I thought, *this lady is a place where God shines through.*

So I presented my gringa-white bottom to her every three days for a series of nine shots. We became very good friends, considering the conversational posture I was required to assume at each visit. I would feel stronger and more animated after each shot. I actually looked forward to taking another blood test to prove I was on the road to recovery.

When I took that test, there was no change. I was still at 8.1. I was officially anemic, and it didn't look as if there was anything I could do about it. I sat in Hummercita, parked in the shade of a fig tree across from the laboratory, and cried. Everything I'd been trying seemed so futile. When I gathered my composure I drove up the hill to Dr. Lidiana's. I thought I was calm, but looking into her eyes I burst into tears once more. She held me and rocked me, speaking softly in Spanish. "They're just numbers. They don't tell you who you really are. God is bigger than this," she assured me. Oh, yeah. That's what I used to tell others. Did I really have a right to think that anymore? That assurance seemed so far away, part of a life that was no longer mine. Would I ever again see myself as a dancing column of light?

I did dance, though, on the advice of another friend. "It gets the heart pumping," she told me, "makes more of that red stuff you need." The Sunday morning after I'd dissolved in Dr. Lidiana's office, I got up mid-morning, fired up iTunes and

189

found George Strait's "All My Exes Live in Texas." It lasts for exactly three minutes and twenty-one seconds, and I gamely two-stepped around the cupola room for the entire duration of every twangy nasal note. When the music stopped, I was seeing stars, fighting to catch my breath and still my pounding heart. I lay back down on the bed and slept hard for three hours.

The day passed in a series of waking and sleeping spells. Sometime that afternoon, the phone rang. It was a call from California. Andy was an old friend with news about a project we'd done together. I listened to him through a groggy stupor. But it was his wife, I realized, with whom I really wanted to talk. In my befogged mental state, I was remembering something. I had a support network. The group of women who had staffed and revolved around Safe Harbor Healing was still intact, now meeting once a week for Bible study. "I need help, Laurie," I confessed, when Andy called her to the phone. "Ask the women to hold me up in thought. Just hold me to the light and keep me in your prayers. Would you all do that for me?" She said she'd get an email out right away.

Wow. I'd asked for help. I'd actually asked for prayers from a group of women who were organized and met regularly— like a church. I hung up the phone and contemplated what I'd done. Looking back I see that moment was the beginning of the end of my railing and chest beating about and against "organized" religion. Just knowing that there were people who loved me unconditionally, who cared for my welfare, and who were "there" for me gave me immense comfort. It was a watershed moment in the whole healing process.

Hadn't I learned this lesson before when I let myself be loved by Larry, when I'd said "yes," and accepted all the love he had to give? When had I become so picky about from where love should come, closing my eyes to the many channels waiting to pour it out on me? Asking that those floodgates be aimed in my direction put a stop to the downward spiraling vortex in which I'd been caught. I felt the current of my life shift.

But there were still rapids ahead. That night I lay awake in agony, and by morning I was making little sense. There didn't seem anything to my being but one big physical sense. Not five, just one, and that one was pain. From the depths of the sleep I'd finally fallen into just before dawn, I prayed not to waken. When I did become conscious, I surfaced leaving behind dreams of how to end my life. I looked at Larry's frightened face, resentful to find myself still living, and broke into sobs.

"I'm calling Ginny," he said.

"I don't care," I responded. I didn't care anymore, and that was a good thing. I didn't care that I'd soon be spilling my guts to a Christian Science practitioner, a Christian Science teacher for that matter, one who I admired, who had mentored me, whose approval I sought as if she were my mother. I didn't care anymore if she knew I'd been consulting doctors, taking addictive painkillers, and thinking about ways to shuffle off the mortal coil. I didn't care what she thought. I didn't care what anyone thought. I'd ceased caring about much of anything at all.

Her voice made me dissolve once more. I lay in bed and sobbed while she told me how much she loved me. Not how much God loved me—how much she loved me. That meant so much more to me. At that moment Ginny was real; God was unknown. She told me she knew who I really was, and how I couldn't fool her into believing I was anything different, no more than she would be fooled by a distorted image in wavy looking glass. She knew me. "What does a trick mirror do but distort our best qualities?" she observed. "What do I think of when I think 'Susan'? Spiritual clarity and strength. Those are the words that come to mind. That's who you are. Don't be fooled. I'm not."

I calmed down to quiet gulps and shallow breaths. *Spiritual clarity and strength?* I thought. Right then that seemed like someone else.

"Take my hand," she directed over the phone. It was a metaphor, and it worked. I was mentally reaching out—a big change. "We'll get through this house of mirrors," she assured me. "I've been through it before. I know the way out."

"You'll work with me?" I gulped. "Even with all this other stuff? Ginny, I can't give up the painkillers right now. I'd go crazy."

"Whatever it takes," she said. "I'm with you. Grab hold. We'll walk through it together. I know who you are, even if you don't."

"Ginny there's *something* there," I insisted. "Something that hurts like hell. My bathroom looks like a war zone. I can't stop bleeding. I want it *out.*"

"Of course you do," she replied. "Whatever it takes."

Dr. Lidiana had referred me to a doctor in Tepic, one of her teachers at the medical school she'd attended, and she had advised me to carry with me the pile of X-rays, studies, DVDs, and blood test results I had amassed over the last few years. "He is a good listener, and he also sees what others do not," she explained.

I had an appointment scheduled for the next day, but Christian Scientists "don't go to doctors." I told Ginny anyway. "I want to keep the appointment," I said. "Will you still work with me even if I do?"

"Whatever it takes," she repeated. "Let him have a look."

Dr. García spoke mostly Spanish and worked out of his own clinic in a less than fashionable area of Tepic. But it was homey and welcoming. His daughter was his receptionist. He was a small fireplug of a man with twinkly eyes that gazed at me through thick lenses. I could easily have rested my chin on his head had we been closer. I sat opposite him, though, and he spread my materials over a battered wooden desk, occasionally asking questions. The vial I'd taken from the desk drawer he glanced at and tossed in the trash. At last he paused, reached for a box of plastic gloves and began pulling on a pair. He switched to English to make himself perfectly clear. "Susie," he said, as though he expected an argument. "I need to see your rrrectoooom."

"At last!" was all I could say.

It didn't take long. His sharp intake of breath told me he saw *something*—something serious enough to refer me immediately to a surgeon. I was with Dr. Cervantes inside of an hour.

This is where I will "cut" to the chase as swiftly as the surgeon decided to cut in my case. Inside a week I was being wheeled into the *quirófono,* the surgery at San Rafael Surgical Center. I will skip details of that week and the several weeks after. There is nothing entertaining, funny, or enlightening about having fifteen hemorrhoids removed. I will say one thing about the procedure and its aftermath: there is nothing more personally inconvenient in the world.

The one slightly surreal moment that warrants a retrospective smile was when the anesthesiologist introduced himself and kept me distracted from the surgery preparations going on around me. Pulling out his iPhone, he flipped through pictures of his family. He was a Huichol Indian, he said, with two wives in the mountain village he called home. There they sat in front of a house on stilts, each dressed in a colorful skirt and blouse, their looms strapped to their backs. *Anchored above,* I thought, thinking how Huichol women begin their weaving by throwing a longitudinal line over a high tree branch. I mentally tossed the warp thread of my life skyward.

"I've mixed a little peyote with the magic serum," he winked at me. "You will have beautiful, colorful dreams. When you wake up it will all be over."

I think he was kidding, at least about the peyote. *Is he really a Huichol?* I wondered. The needle was in the IV, and I was fading. I'd give him a test.

"How do you pronounce *w-i-x-i-r-i-k-a?*" I asked. He answered, but I don't remember what he said. He was right. When I woke up, it was all over.

It was a short stay in the hospital, nothing like the times before. I was in on Thursday, out on Saturday. The surgeon visited me before I left. "All gone!" he assured me, raising a jar of—yeesh, I didn't want to look—to prove it. I set about recovering, both physically and spiritually. Ginny was on the phone with me every step of the way.

Four weeks later on a trip to the States, I saw her for real. I'd run up ramps in airports, hiked miles to go through customs, and pulled around a bag heavy with winter clothing for New England. There was no pain, no shortness of breath or starry-eyed dizziness. Even my fingernails were nice and rosy once more. As I reached for the hand she'd held out to me over the phone, she enveloped me in a big hug.

"It's over," I said. "Thank you! I know who I am again."

FOCAL POINT

[Virginity] is something I carry very deep within, that I
carry very secretly … virginity is centered in the heart
and could be named 'singleness of heart.' Virginity is a
state that returns to God in wholeness. This wholeness is
not that of having experienced all experiences, but of
something reserved, preserved, or reclaimed for what it
was made for. Virginity is the ability to stay centered,
with oneness of purpose.

Words of a Benedictine sister,
quoted by Kathleen Norris in *The Cloister Walk*

CHAPTER 17

QUERIDA VIRGENCITA

This is the word which [Love] hath spoken
concerning him [that oppressed thee]; The virgin,
the daughter of Zion, hath despised [your oppressor],
and laughed [him] to scorn.

Isaiah

Dear Susan,

Maybe I should say *"Querida Susana,"* instead. You're ten years old, almost eleven. You've been to Mexico City, seen the Virgin, and are eager to learn Spanish. Keep at it! It will be one of the most valuable assets of your life.

I'm writing to you as a child, knowing you'll grow up to be me. Weird, huh? But my friend Penelope, whose job it is to make families better and who does it so well, said it might be a good idea to try this. She said maybe you could use a friend from the future at this time of your life.

Something has changed this summer, hasn't it? You're not the confident conquer-the-world young lady that you were last summer when you discovered Mexico, when you came face to face with Guadalupe for the very first time. Something has thrown you off balance, and I know you don't want to talk

197

about it. You won't talk about it, because—well, there is no reason. There never is. It's literally unspeakable. Your mouth won't form the words.

Let's take a closer look at that hard, dark place in your heart that you've been hiding. What you think is an ugly secret may turn out to be something else entirely. If there's anyone who would understand, it's me, and I can tell you our most unpleasant, shame-filled experiences carry the potential to transform us. Having just experienced that kind of healing, I'm inclined to spread it around, not only into my future, but reaching back to you, too, so far in the past. Let's see if we can't take that knobby, dark-hued seedpod of a secret and watch it germinate into something grand—maybe a tenacious, flowering vine that will wander through your life and perfume the air around it. When people see—when you see in yourself—this amazing power and beauty, there will be no memory of the ugly little lump that was. It will be gone, dissolved. What we need, though, is some proper soil.

Okay. Here's the down and dirty. There are some old men who touch and fondle young girls, who perform acts that are horrible and make you ashamed. It is not your fault, and you are not alone. My friend Penelope tells me that as many as one in every four women has been sexually molested in childhood, almost always by someone they know. But no matter how common, no matter how often it happens, it happened to you, and as another friend of mine says, "It really messes with your head."

Sweetheart, let me tell you something. You are completely innocent. I want you to know that now, even if you didn't know it then. I can assure you from this distance, this fifty years in the future looking back, that the essence of what you are has always been safe. It could never be touched, never be sullied. Nothing any old man could ever do to you could stop your being the image of the "one-in-herself" virgin who Mother God conceived you to be.

May I tell you how proud I am of you and how pretty I think you are? Your parents don't want to spoil you, don't want to put prideful thoughts in your head, so they don't tell you that too often. How little they realize how uncertain you are these days, how the smart mouth, know-it-all, "let me do it myself" outward bravado you exhibit hides a young girl who's desperately afraid of being left far behind. Your friends have started telling jokes that you don't "get," though you laugh louder than any one of them. When you do get an explanation, it seems totally incredible.

Oh, what wouldn't I do for you now! Together we'd kick that old man right in the balls, yell at him for putting his hands where they don't belong. We'd run out to the lifeguard at the pool and shout out loud what was happening. Then together we'd scream *Hah!* at the top of our lungs and demand that he stop, no matter his name, no matter his reputation, no matter what other people thought. How dare he make you afraid! He's the one who should be trembling in his spectator shoes, because you are the one with the power.

Then, when things got all calmed down, we'd catch our breath and look at each other. It's good, isn't it, to have a friend you can count on? I'd explain those stupid jokes to you, and maybe we'd laugh. Maybe we'd just shrug and say, "That's dumb." But, little friend, you aren't dumb at all. There is nothing wiser than innocence. In your own special way you are a *marisabia*. That's a new word I've learned. In Spanish it means "Mary Sage." People use it to describe women who "know it all," I suppose because there were so many Marys in the Bible who were smarter than the men around them. Like Mary Baker Eddy was smart, and Sor Juan Inés de la Cruz was smart. There have been a lot of smart women, *marisabias*, throughout history, though you won't learn about them in school. I've come to know them for myself over these past ten years or so, and I like to think that they're my friends now—and, of course, that would make them your friends, too! We *marisabias* need to stick together.

And, Susana, *virgencita*. I would make every birthday special for you, bake the kind of cake you like, and invite all your friends to celebrate. Not everything your mother tells you is accurate. I can have my own opinions now, and my opinion is: You're never too old to have a party. With what I know now, in a few years when you turn fifteen, I would give you a *quincianera*— hire a band, have a big party, and put a crown on your head. Every girl should be a princess at some time in her life, and the earlier she knows how to wear a crown, the more in control of her life she is. Doesn't the Queen of Heaven, Guadalupe herself, wear a crown some days? Every woman should have at least one in her wardrobe. I got mine last summer when I turned sixty. My friend Ann bought *quincianera* paraphernalia and then put a big "x 4" beside every number "15." It's never too late to claim your crown.

Don't give up on your passions and talents, *querida*. Don't let anyone make fun of the fact that you love to read, that you write secret journals. Keep those journals. Record every detail that attracts your eye. It is not a waste of time. Do what you love doing, not what is practical. Not everything has to serve an immediate purpose. Most of the time it's the process that matters, not the thing you produce. Write! Draw! Paint! Sing! Dance! It's never too early or too late to express yourself completely. You drew fearlessly before this last summer, but you set it aside, unsure of yourself, fearful of not being "good" enough. I draw for us now, painting pictures of the Virgin, of *catrinas,* of flowers and trees and of the wonderful landscapes around me. Faces I paint, of women who know things, of women whom I'd like to know.

You used to sing, *querida,* performing, and dancing, lip-synching, and vamping. "Don't be a show off," they'd say. "Don't be silly." So afraid you would embarrass them, so afraid you'd make a fool of yourself. Listen, my friend, it's foolish *not* to sing, crazy *not* to dance. I sing now with all my heart—and perform without my knees knocking together.

And, yes, I pose for pictures, *querida.* I'm not afraid anymore, because I know we're beautiful. I know how difficult it was with Daddy. He wanted you to be his perfect angel: "Don't smirk," he'd say. "Smile! Come on," he'd say. "You call that a smile? Let's have a real smile. Smile like you mean it." My smile isn't forced these days, dear heart, even though there are a lot more "smile lines" around it.

Do you remember how just a year ago when you were nine, you could stand on one leg and pivot around? Mom called you "the stork," because it seemed natural to you to stand that way—spine straight, shoulders back, perfectly balanced and free. You haven't tried it lately, have you? Not only does the

201

kind of intrusion like at the swimming pool mess with your head, it puts you off balance physically.

But hey, I've got it back for us! It came to me in yoga sessions out beside our pool here in Mexico. It was embarrassing for me at first. I couldn't even place the sole of one foot against the ankle of the other without wobbling and falling over. But it was thinking of you that changed everything. One morning it came to me: it shouldn't just be me trying to help that ten-year-old I once was. Turnabout is fair play. That ten-year-old could help me. I stepped back to the Mexico City summer and thought of you—that innocent "I can do anything" nine-year-old you with the perfect posture and poise. I felt a mental shift. I found myself moving into a perfect tree pose, sole of my foot planted against my thigh, solid, secure, my hands reaching for the sky. What joy! No wobbles! We've got our balance back!

Your life is in balance, whether you know it or not, *querida*. You've got a mom and dad who love you a lot, even if they seem absolutely incompetent at the task sometimes. Remember, they're doing their very best. After all, you're their first. You didn't exactly come with an instruction manual. Both of them, they're the youngest ones of great big families. Don't you think their brothers and sisters thought they were spoiled? Don't you think they'd do anything to keep you from being called the same? They want you to be perfect, for everyone to love you as much as they do, so they don't tell you how wonderful you are. Ah, but I will spoil you now! I will heap praise on you, as well as the "crown in heaven reserved for you"—I will snatch it down from the skies and place it on your head. Guadalupe knows you need it now.

You'll come to know Guadalupe better some day, but for now be glad of the religion you have. It's different, I know, and sometimes it gets very lonely. But there are good differences you're going to grow up with. You're going to learn by example—that girls can know God and talk about the Bible with just as much authority as any boy or man. You're going to get a good education on that Bible, so you can thump back at those Bible-thumpers who would thump you down. You're going to get brazen sometimes. Growing up "different," you won't be afraid to make a difference. Yeah, sometimes you'll fall flat on your face. It happens.

Now, let's talk about your body. I know you've grown touchy. You flinch when anyone reaches out for you. You've begun hunching forward, curling inward, self-conscious and shy, trying to hide your height. The next thing you'll be trying to hide is that flat little chest. What can I say? You're never going to have big boobs. Trust me on this, *querida*. That's just the way it is. But there's nothing to be ashamed of at all. In a few years, buy a bikini and wear it! You are not going to have that flat stomach forever. Take advantage of it *now*.

There will come a time when you won't be so touchy and shy. I promise you that. You're going to meet a wonderfully patient man, and you're going to love him like crazy and want him to touch you all over. I know. He's here with me now and sends you his love. He is living proof that kind and gentle men are out there. They cherish women who have a strong sense of themselves and what they stand for. It can be as much a struggle for these wonderful guys as it is for us girls and women to maintain that tender strength, that attitude of listening, that sets standards for civilization. But just like Mary had her

Joseph, I do believe that everyone should have someone who will be there loving and supporting us as we carry out what we are meant to do in life. They'll do it without trying to possess us. Be careful to whom you give your heart. Make sure it's to someone who will be there in your corner, cheering you on as you fulfill your dreams and accomplish all of which you're capable. But, hey! Look who I'm talking to! You know this intuitively. Because you did it!

Now *querida,* come with me back to Mexico and take a look at what's right at the center of our cupola room. Yep! I did it. I posed for David Delgadillo, that artist who had the show of painted body forms at Xaltemba. Small boobs, *panzona,* and all, I did it. That is my naked torso standing there on the cedar chest, surrounded by books, and mirrors, and all the colorful stuff from the *tianguis.* It was Larry's idea, and how could I deny him? We did it the day after Christmas, and the finished piece was delivered in time for his birthday in March.

I had to shave every inch, every *centímetro,* of my body so David and María Isabel could apply the plaster strips. No, silly, not the hair on my head. This is a torso like the Venus de Milo we're talking about, no arms or legs, and definitely not a head. It's just the core of my body, the center part. To do it, we went up to the studio on the roof, close to the sky and the birds. It took about an hour, as David and María dipped long white strips of cloth into plaster of Paris and covered me completely from my thighs to my neck. I had my arms raised, supported by ski poles. As they worked, the plaster cast around me got heavier and heavier. I'd been cold at first, but it was warm in that cast as it dried. What a weird suction-y feeling I got as it dried and pulled away from my skin. It was funny looking, *querida*. You would have laughed and laughed. Larry and I did, because, of course, he was right there by my side.

Never would I have thought I could do such a thing—handing my body over in such a way, being absolutely naked in front of other people. Perhaps it was those times in the hospital, being poked and prodded, examined and explored in ways I'd never imagined I'd ever willingly tolerate. It was all so new to me, you know, that whole hospital thing. Letting myself be put to sleep and going into surgery, having confidence that people I barely knew would take good care of me—that was a major step forward in the faith department for me. I haven't ever trusted anyone like that. Not since that old man stuff.

I suppose there's a point in everyone's life where we just have to get over it, let loose of who we think we are or what we think has happened to us. That's the only way we can be free to be something totally new. All that we have of the past is our present concept of it. So that's the way I approached this statue situation. It was an opportunity to be something new, to look at my body in a whole different way.

That torso of me in the cupola is a celebration, an *agradecimiento* like the ones in the Basilica of Guadalupe that you saw last summer or the ones I saw last year at the shrine in Talpa. It is beautiful, a true work of art. It looks like I'm covered in gold-plated armor etched with wonderful colors. There are mandalas and runes, and a great sun shining out of my belly, and on the other side a series of circles across my shoulders and another mandala in the small of my back. Worked into the background there are *ohm* symbols, which mean mother, and there is also the pink flower pattern the Virgin of Guadalupe wears on her gown. I look at it and I see you, I see me, and I see my mother, all rolled up into one. There are symbols representing all three, but all of us are one.

There's also a surprise symbol on the torso. I thought I was mistaken when I first saw it, but as I looked more closely, I knew exactly what it was.

"Did you see what is between the breasts?" David asked me. It was a few weeks after I got the statue that I saw him again. "She just appeared there," he said apologetically. "I'm not Catholic, and I know you're not either. I tried to make her go away, but in the end I had to leave her."

There she is, *querida,* a tiny image of Guadalupe, wrapped in a blue cloak to match the angels that he's painted at the base of each of my legs.

"That's all right," I told him. "I know she belongs there."

She does belong there, Susan, my child, myself, there in our heart as she has been forever, She is the truth of who you are and always will be, *querida virgencita.* She is what I am—the image of God.

EPILOGUE

It's never "all over," is it? The road goes on forever, with all its bends and twists. Sometimes it may seem to end in a cul-de-sac with no way out. But right there, in a dead end space, my particular *calle sin salida* turned into a *retorno*.

Because everything turns us back to love, doesn't it? In every rotten experience, every disappointed hope, there's a lesson in love waiting to be learned. Most of the time it's not so much about giving love as it is receiving it. Probably the most difficult thing any of us ever faces is opening up and being known for what we are. To do it, and then find we're loved in spite of it all, that's the spiritual ideal.

Love is always there, though at first blush we may not recognize it for what it is. The Virgin is like that. She'll fool you with those downcast eyes, that quietness of just "being there." But steadfastly being one-in-one's-self, un-captured, un-invaded, intact, self-complete, innocent—that's a power that can change the world. It changed mine. Continues to change it.

Look for the Virgin. You might find her presiding over the altar in a church somewhere. Or not. She may be standing out on some jetty facing down the waves, covered in salt spray and plastic flowers. More likely, she'll be working with an alias—like Larry or Ginny, Mom or Dad, Dr. So-and-So, the neighbor next door. She could even be the neighbor on the other side of the world. The Virgin has always been there, will always be there, in one form or another. She comes in all genders, ages, and sizes. But there's always one place you're sure to find Her.

Look in the mirror.

ACKNOWLEDGEMENTS

Thanks, first of all, to the original gang of editors at spirituality.com, who let me write about soul-touching issues in a funny and frank way. Virginia Harris, Chris Raymond, Mario Tosto, Laura Matthews, Carol Winograd – you helped me find my voice.

Thank you to all who read my blog and asked, "So why don't you write a book?" You gave me courage to start.

Thanks to patient friends who waded through early drafts or listened while painting, dining, driving or sharing sleeping quarters on various adventures. You asked probing questions that demanded deep self-examination, and insisted I write from an honest heart. You gave me courage to keep going.

Thanks to Penelope and Penny, Tosia and Trish, for valuable input and proofing. Thanks Carol Hohle for taking it from manuscript to book form. And thanks especially to you, Laura Matthews, story analyst and editor *extraordinaire*.

Thank you, Carol and Bernard, for shelter and counsel in the big cold city. Thank you, Molly Boyle, wherever you are. You were once at Bantam, listened to my incoherent heartfelt pitch and said "Send me a synopsis and the first fifty pages." I didn't *have* them! I regret that missed opportunity, but you let me know that what I had in mind could be a real book. Here it is.

Thank you, Ginny, for everything. You know what that includes.

And thank you, Larry, for being who you are, and always being there.

Source Material

Anderson, Carl and Eduardo Chavez. *Our Lady of Guadalupe.* New York: Doubleday, 2009.

Arenal, Electa and Amanda Powell. *Sor Juana Inés de la Cruz: The Answer/ La Respuesta, Including a Selection of Poems.* New York: The Feminist Press at the City University of New York, 1994.

Bundesen, Lynne. *The Feminine Spirit: Recapturing the Heart of Scripture.* Hoboken, NJ: John Wiley and Sons, 2007.

Castillo, Ana, editor. *Goddess of The Americas: Writings on the Virgin of Guadalupe.* New York: Riverhead Books, 1996.

Eddy, Mary Baker. *Science and Health with Key to the Scriptures.* Boston: The Writings of Mary Baker Eddy, 1910.

—. *In My True Light and Life.* Boston: The Writings of Mary Baker Eddy and The Mary Baker Eddy Library for the Betterment of Humanity, 2002.

Garcia Samper, Asunción, et. al. *El Santo Juan Diego: El Mensajero Indígena de la Virgen de Guadalupe.* México, D.F.: Centro de Estudios Mesoamericanos, A.C., 2002.

Gill, Gillian. *Mary Baker Eddy.* Reading, MA: Perseus Books, 1998.

Harding, M. Esther. *Woman's Mysteries Ancient and Modern.* New York: Harper and Row, 1971.

Johnson, Elizabeth A. *Quest for the Living God: Mapping Frontiers in the Theology of God*. New York: The Continuum International Publishing Group, Inc., 2007.

—. *She Who Is*. New York: The Crossroad Publishing Company, 1998

Kidd, Sue Monk. *The Dance of the Dissident Daughter*. New York: Harper Collins, 2002.

Norris, Kathleen. *The Cloister Walk*. New York: Riverhead Books, 1996.

—. *The Quotidien Mysteries*. Mahwah, NJ: Paulist Press, 1998.

Rodriguez, Jeanette. *Our Lady of Guadalupe: Faith and Empowerment among Mexican-American Women*. Austin: University of Texas Press, 1994.

Schaefer, Stacey. *To Think With a Good Heart: Wixarika Women, Weavers, and Shamans*. Salt Lake City: The University of Utah Press, 2002.

Spong, John Shelby. *Why Christianity Must Change or Die: A Bishop Speaks to Believers in Exile*. San Francisco: HarperOne, 1998.

READING GROUP GUIDE
AND
TOPICS FOR DISCUSSION

1. The word virgin has a variety of definitions, including *fresh, new, unadulterated, native, uncaptured, unexplored.* How might these and other meanings apply literally and metaphorically to the journey described in *Virgin Territory?* Does the book depict more than one journey?

2. West Texas is referred to as having masculine geography, while the area of Mexico in which the book is set is described as feminine. What contrasts does the author draw between the two? What other attributes of the Mexican landscape and culture does she see as distinctly feminine? Do you think topography and climate affect the mental outlook of a population? If so, give examples.

3. *No da color* is a Mexican euphemism for failure to define oneself or take definitive action. What definitive actions does the author take in redefining herself? What feminine

icons or role models does she find helpful in doing this? Can you remember a specific instance when you have taken definitive action to identify yourself in a new way? Have feminine role models or icons been helpful to you? If so, which ones?

4. Human beings tend to form communities around common interests or necessities. These communities might be intentional, or they may evolve more informally. What are some of the communities to which the author belonged? In what ways were they supportive? What communities do you find supportive in your own experience? Is there a time when it is expedient to leave a community? What might precipitate such action?

5. The author refers to being "pissed off at patriarchy," yet she dedicates *Virgin Territory* to her husband. To what is she alluding when she uses the term "patriarchy"? What particular traits or characteristics might be identified as "patriarchal?" Are these traits the exclusive province of men, or can women, as well, be patriarchal?

6. That Deity has an ancient feminine face and nature is a major theme throughout *Virgin Territory*. Does that face have different aspects? In what ways might finding the feminine face of God affect the way individuals deal with themselves and others? Would it change the way one might pray? In what ways might a more feminine spiritual ideal affect societies and nations?

ABOUT THE AUTHOR

Susan J. Cobb has toured extensively throughout the United States and Mexico, speaking on practical spirituality and the role of women in religion. Also a well-known author of inspirational articles, Cobb makes her first foray into books with *Virgin Territory*. She lives with her husband in Mexico.

4778307R0

Made in the USA
Charleston, SC
15 March 2010